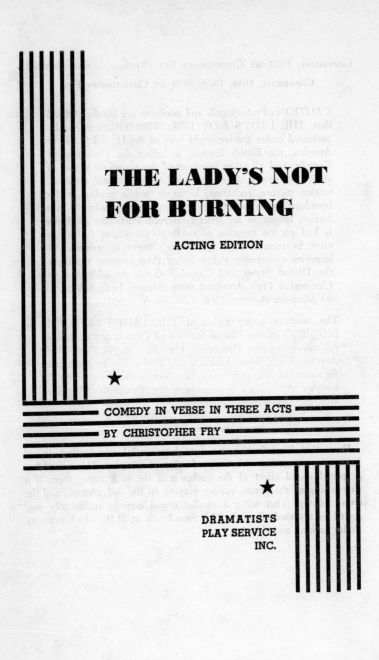

THE LADY'S NOT FOR BURNING

ACTING EDITION

★

COMEDY IN VERSE IN THREE ACTS

BY CHRISTOPHER FRY

★

**DRAMATISTS
PLAY SERVICE
INC.**

SOUND EFFECT RECORD

Dramatists Play Service can furnish a special sound effect record for use in connection with the production of this play. This record has a special sound effect of the cuckoo and the cock crow; there is a chorus singing the hymn; various playing on the viol; chimes; and the crowd offstage (but using a smaller crowd may be realistically suggested by a crowd offstage). This record sells at $3.80, which price includes packing and shipping.

THE LADY'S NOT FOR BURNING was first produced in New York City by Atlantis Productions (The Theatre Guild—Tennent Productions Ltd.—John C. Wilson) at the Royale Theatre, November 8, 1950. It was directed by John Gielgud, and the decor was by Oliver Messel. The cast was as follows:

RICHARD, an orphaned clerk ....Richard Burton
THOMAS MENDIP, a discharged soldier ....John Gielgud
ALIZON ELIOT ....Penelope Munday
NICHOLAS DEVISE ....David Evans
MARGARET DEVISE, mother of Nicholas..............Nora Nicholson
HUMPHREY DEVISE, brother of Nicholas..............Richard Leech
HEBBLE TYSON, the Mayor..........................George Howe
JENNET JOURDEMAYNE ....Pamela Brown
THE CHAPLAIN ....Eliot Makeham
EDWARD TAPPERCOOM, a justice........................Peter Bull
MATTHEW SKIPPS ....Esmé Percy

SCENE

A room in the house of Hebble Tyson, Mayor of the small market town of Cool Clary.

TIME

The 15th Century, either more or less or exactly.

ACT I
An afternoon in April.

ACT II
An hour later.

ACT III
Later, the same night.

THE LADY'S NOT FOR BURNING

ACT I

The scene is a room in the house of HEBBLE TYSON, *Mayor of the little market town of Cool Clary, in England. The scene and the appearance of the characters are as much Fifteenth Century as anything. A photograph of the stage is reproduced in the frontispiece of this book. The large window up-stage is used to a great extent as an entrance, the shutters standing open. To R. and L., just below the window, are stone benches, referred to in stage directions as "sills." Across the stage, extending from the stone buttress U. R. to a similar buttress U. L., is a raised platform. While this may not prove to be necessary, it will be found effective in many scenes, since the actors often use it to sit on. To L. of this platform is another platform U. L., on which stands a crude wooden desk, behind which is a chair. Against the pillar L., about four feet above the floor is a lectern, and attached to it an inkwell and quill pen. In the U. L. corner of the room L. of the pillar, an open entrance, at the top of a flight of three or four steps which leads to two other apartments off stage. Somewhat below this open entrance is a low door—just barely perceptible in the photograph—which leads to the cellar. To R. of the C. window, and somewhat below it, at an angle from U. C. to D. R. is the door to the study. D. R. of the R. buttress is a short passageway leading up to a door, which stands open, and leads to the garden. About C. stage is a chair, L. stage, a stool, and R., to L. of R. buttress, another stool. Below this stool is a fairly long, crude wooden bench. Just below this bench is an iron cooking pot, and*

*below that, somewhat to the L. of it, a small pile of fire-
wood. The sticks of wood are more symbolic than actual,
and the fire is not practical.*

As the curtain rises RICHARD, *a young copying clerk, is
sitting on the L. window seat, eating.*

THOMAS. (*Off, calls.*)

    Soul!

(RICHARD *rises hurriedly, crosses to rostrum by desk, picks up
book, places it on lectern L., starts to write.*)

RICHARD.

    . . . and the plasterer, that's fifteen pence . . .

THOMAS.

    Hey, soul!

RICHARD.

    . . . for stopping the draught in the privy . . .

THOMAS. (*Appears in window R.*)

    Body!

    You calculating piece of clay.

(*Enters through open window C., stands on R. window sill.*)

RICHARD.

    Damnation!

THOMAS.

    Don't mention it. I've never seen a world
    So festering with damnation. I have left
    Rings of beer on every alehouse table
    From the salt sea coast across half a dozen counties,
    But each time I thought I was on the way
    To a faintly festive hiccup
    The sight of the damned world sobered me up again.
    (*Crosses to below desk.*)
    Where is the Mayor? I've business with His Worship.

RICHARD.

    Where have you come from?

THOMAS.

    Straight from your alehouse.
    Damnation's pretty active there this afternoon,
    Licking her lips over gossip of murder and witchcraft.
    There's mischief brewing for someone. Where's the Mayor?

RICHARD.

I'm the Mayor's clerk.

THOMAS.

How are you?

(*They shake hands.*)

RICHARD.

Can I have your name?

THOMAS.

It's yours.

RICHARD.

Now, look . . .

THOMAS.

It's no earthly
Use to me. I travel light; as light,
That is, as a man can travel who will
Still carry his body around because
Of its sentimental value.

(*Sits on rostrum below desk.*)

Flesh
Weighs like a thousand years, and every morning
Wakes heavier for an intake of uproariously
Comical dreams which smell of henbane,
Guts, humors, ventricles, nerves, fibres,
And fat . . . the arterial labyrinth, body's hell.
Still, it was the first thing my mother gave me,
God rest her soul. What were you saying?

RICHARD.

Name

And business.

(*This time he crosses to lectern, picks up pen, starts to write.*)

THOMAS.

Thomas Mendip. My well-born father,
If birth can ever be said to be well, maintains
A castle as draughty as a tree. At every sunset
It falls, reflecting down into the river, and fish swim
Through its walls. They swim into the bosom of my grand-
    mother,
Who sits late, watching for the constellation of Orion
Because my dead grandfather, she believes,
is situated somewhere in the Belt.

7

That is part of the glory of my childhood.

RICHARD.

I like you as much as I've liked anybody.

(THOMAS *laughs*.)

Perhaps you're a little drunk. But here, I'm afraid,
They may not take to you.

THOMAS. (*Moves to chair* C.)

That's what I hope.

RICHARD.

Who told you to come here?
You couldn't have chosen a less fortunate afternoon.
They're expecting company . . . well, a girl. Excuse me,
I must get back to the books.

(*Moves* L.)

THOMAS. (*Sits chair* C.)

I'll wait.

RICHARD.

He'll not

See anybody; I'm sure of it.

(*Back to* L. *of* THOMAS.)

THOMAS.

Dear boy,

I only want to be hanged. What possible
Objection can he have to that?

RICHARD.

Why no, I . . .

To be . . . *want* to be hanged? How very drunk you are,
After all. Who ever would want to be hanged?

THOMAS.

You don't

Make any allowance for individuality.
How do you know that out there, in the day or night,
According to latitude, the entire world
Isn't wanting to be hanged? Now you, for instance,
Still damp from your cocoon, you're desperate
To fly into any noose of the sun that should dangle
Down from the sky. Life, forbye, is the way

(*Rises, goes behind chair* C.)

We fatten for the Michaelmas of our own particular
Gallows.—

8

What a wonderful thing is metaphor!

(Knock on door U. L.)

RICHARD.

Was that a knock?

THOMAS. (To U. C.)

The girl. She knocks. I saw her
Walking in the garden beside a substantial nun.
Whsst! Revelation!

(Enter ALIZON ELIOT, aged seventeen, talking to herself, from
door U. L.)

ALIZON. (Coming down steps to stage level.)

Two steps down, she said. One, two,
The floor. Now I begin to be altogether
Different . . . I suppose.

RICHARD.

Oh, God, God,
God, God, God! I can see such trouble!
Is life sending a flame to nest in my flax?
For pity's sake!

THOMAS.

Sweet pretty noose, nice noose.

(Goes to window seat.)

RICHARD. (Steps toward ALIZON.)

Will you step in?

ALIZON. (Turns to RICHARD.)

They told me no one was here.

RICHARD.

It would be me they meant.

ALIZON.

Oh, would it be?
Coming in from the light, I am all out at the eyes.
(Crosses to chair C.)
Such white doves were paddling in the sunshine
And the trees were as bright as a shower of broken glass.
Out there, in the sparkling air, the sun and the rain
Clash together like the cymbals clashing
When David did his dance.
(Hand over her eyes.)

I've an April blindness.
You're hidden in a cloud of crimson catherine-wheels.

9

RICHARD.

It doesn't really matter. Sit in the shadow.

THOMAS.

There are plenty to choose from.

ALIZON.

Oh, there are three of us.

(Makes small curtsey to THOMAS, *moves behind bench* R.)
Forgive me.

RICHARD. *(Moves* U. *to below desk.)*

He's waiting . . . he wants . . . he says . . .

(Laughs. ALIZON *goes round* R. *end of bench* R. *to front of it.)*
THOMAS.

I breathe,

I spit, I am. But take no further notice.
I'll just nod in at the window like a rose;
I'm a black and frosted rosebud whom the good God
Has preserved since last October. Take no notice.

(Sits on L. *window seat.)*
ALIZON.

Men, to me, are a world to themselves.

RICHARD.

Do you think so?

ALIZON.

I am going to be married to one of them, almost at once.
I have met him already.

RICHARD.

Humphrey, the Town Councillor.

ALIZON.

Are you his brother?

RICHARD.

No. All I can claim as my flesh and blood
Is what I stand up in. I wasn't born,
I was come-across. In the dusk of one Septuagesima,
A priest found an infant, about ten inches long,
Crammed into the poor-box. The money had all
Been taken. Nothing was there except myself,
I was the baby, as it turned out. The priest,
Thinking I might have eaten the money, held me
Upside down and shook me, which encouraged me
To live, I suppose, and I lived.

10

(Crosses behind bench to R. *of it.)*

ALIZON.

No father or mother?

RICHARD. *(Sits* R. *of* ALIZON *on bench.)*
Not noticeably.

ALIZON.
You mustn't let it make you conceited.
Pride is one of the deadly sins.

THOMAS.
And it's better to go for the lively ones.

ALIZON.
Which ones

Do you mean?

THOMAS.
Pay no heed. I was nodding in.

ALIZON.
I am quite usual, with five elder sisters. My birth
Was a great surprise to my parents, I think. There had been
A misunderstanding and I appeared overnight
As mushrooms do. It gave my father thrombosis.
He thought he would never be able to find enough husbands
For six of us, and so he made up his mind
To simplify matters, and let me marry God.
He gave me to a convent.

RICHARD.
What showing did he think he would make as God's
Father-in-law?

ALIZON.
He let his beard grow longer.
But he found that husbands fell into my sister's laps.
So then he stopped thinking of God as eligible . . .
No prospects, he thought. And he looked around and found
me
Humphrey Devize. Do you think he will do?

RICHARD.
Maybe.

He isn't God, of course.

ALIZON.
No, he isn't.

He's very nearly black.

11

RICHARD.

                         Swarthy.
ALIZON.

                                        Is that it?
When he dies it may be hard to picture him
Agreeable to the utter white of heaven.
Now you, you are . . .
RICHARD.

                              Purgatory-color.
ALIZON.

   It's on the way to grace. Who are you?
RICHARD. (*Rising.*)

                                   Richard,
   The Mayor's copying clerk.
(*Crosses behind bench to door* U. L.)
ALIZON.

                         The Mayor is Humphrey's
Uncle. Humphrey's mother is the Mayor's sister.
And then, again, there's Nicholas, Humphrey's brother.
Is he sensible?
RICHARD.

              He knows his way about.
THOMAS.

   O enviable Nick.
RICHARD.

               He's nodding in.
ALIZON. (*Sits stool* D. L. RICHARD *sits steps* D. L.)
   I'll tell you a strange thing. Humphrey Devize
   Came to the convent to see me, bringing a present
   For his almost immediate wife, he said, which is me,
   Of barley sugar and a cross of seed pearls. Next day
   Nicholas came, with a little cold pie, to say
   He had a message from Humphrey. And then he sat
   And stared and said nothing until he got up to go.
   I asked him for the message, but by then
   It had gone out of his head. Quite gone, you see.
   It was curious. . . . Now you're not speaking either.
RICHARD. (*Rises.*)
   Yes, of course; it was curious.

                         12

ALIZON.

    Men are strange. It's almost unexpected
    To find they speak English. Do you think so too?

RICHARD.

    Things happen to them.

ALIZON.

                      What things?

RICHARD.

                              Machinations of nature;
    As April does to the earth.

ALIZON.

                        I wish it were true!
    Show me daffodils happening to a man!

RICHARD.

    Very easily.

THOMAS.

               And thistles as well, and ladies
    Bedstraw and deadly nightshade, and the need
    For rhubarb.

ALIZON.

           Is it a riddle?

RICHARD.

                   Very likely.
    Certainly a considerable complication.

(NICHOLAS DEVIZE *enters from* U. R. *carrying a horoscope—written on piece of paper—running down-stage, calling as he comes.*)

NICHOLAS.

    Where are you, Alizon?
    (*Sees her and crosses to her.*)
                 Alizon, what do you think?
    (ALIZON *rises.*)
    The stars have blown all my way, by Providence!
    It's me you're going to marry. What do you think
    Of that?

RICHARD.

          You have mud in your mouth.

NICHOLAS.

                       You canter off.

ALIZON.

    No, Nicholas. That's untrue. I have to be

The wife of Humphrey.

NICHOLAS.

Heaven says no. The stars
Say Alizon for Nicholas, Nicholas for Alizon.

RICHARD. (*Moves down* L.)

Are you mad? Why don't you
Go and clean yourself up?

NICHOLAS.

What shall I do
With this nattering wheygoose, Alizon?
Shall I knock him down?

ALIZON.

His name is Richard, he says;
And I think he might knock you down.

(NICHOLAS *crosses to* RICHARD, *his fists at the ready*.)

THOMAS.

Nicholas,
He might. There you have a might for once
That's right. Forgive me, an unwarranted interruption.

NICHOLAS.

Come in, come in. Alizon dear, this Richard
Is all very well. But I was conceived as a hammer
And born in a rising wind.

(*Hands horoscope to* R. *of* ALIZON.)

I apologize
For boasting, but once you know my qualities
I can drop back into a quite brilliant
Humility. God have mercy on me,

(ALIZON *rises.* NICHOLAS *takes her hands.*)

You have such little hands. I knew I should love you.

(MARGARET DEVIZE *enters from study door* R., *carrying her
sewing.* RICHARD *sees her, goes back to lectern.*)

How long will it be before you love me, Alizon?
Let's go.

RICHARD. (*To* ALIZON.)

Just tell me: am I to knock him down? You have only
To say so.

ALIZON.

No, oh, no. We only have
To be patient and unweave him. He is mixed,

14

Aren't you, Nicholas?

NICHOLAS.

                              Compounded of all combustibles,
The world's inside. I'm the receipt God followed
In the creation. It took the roof off his oven.
How long will it be before you love me, Alizon?
Let's go.

(NICHOLAS *picks* ALIZON *up and runs across* R. *with her.* MARGARET
has shut study door and takes step down-stage.)

MARGARET.

Where are you taking Alizon, Nicholas?

NICHOLAS.

Out into the air, Mother.

MARGARET.

                              Unnecessary.
She's in the air already. This room is full of it.
Put her down, Nicholas.

(NICHOLAS *puts* ALIZON *down on bench* R. *of fire—i.e. sticks
on floor below* R. *bench.*)

                              You look
As though you had come straight out of a wheelbarrow;
And not even straight out. And the air so trim
And fresh. It's such a pity.

NICHOLAS.

                    I must tell you,
I've just been reborn.

MARGARET.

                    Nicholas, you always think
You can do things better than your mother. You can be sure
You were born quite adequately on the first occasion.

(NICHOLAS *sits on stool* L. MARGARET *sees* THOMAS *and crosses
to bench* R.)

There is someone here I don't know. Who is it, Alizon?
Did he come with you?

ALIZON. (*Goes to* MARGARET.)

Oh, no. A rosebud, he says.

MARGARET.

A rosebud, Alizon?

ALIZON.

                    He budded in October.

15

MARGARET.

    He's not speaking the truth.
(Sits on bench with ALIZON.)

               . . . You're a pretty child,
And mercifully without spots, unlike
The cowslip. Oh, heavens, we've all been young,
Young all day long, young in and out of season,
In the dream, in the glass, in the firelight—
Perfectly young, obstreperously golden.
What a martyrdom it was.
(Looks toward window.)

               . . . Tch! More rain!

This is properly April.
(To ALIZON.)

            And you're eager to see
Your handsome Humphrey. Nicholas will fetch him.
They're inseparable, really twin natures, utterly
Brothers, like the two ends of the same thought—
Nicholas dear, call Humphrey.

NICHOLAS.

               I can't. I've killed him.

MARGARET.

    Fetch Humphrey, Nicholas dear.

NICHOLAS.

               I've killed him, dearest
Mother.

MARGARET.

    Well, never mind. Call Humphrey, dear.
(Patting ALIZON's *cheek.)*

THOMAS. *(Looking out of window to* R.)
    Is that the other end of this happy thought,
There, prone in the flower bed?

RICHARD. *(Looks out of window.)*

             Yes, it's Humphrey
Lying in the rain.

MARGARET.

           One day I shall burst my bud
Of calm, and blossom into hysteria.
Tell him to get up. Why on this patient earth
Is he lying in the rain?

16

THOMAS.

All flesh is grass.

(Sits on L. window seat. Exit RICHARD U. R.)

ALIZON.

Have you really killed Humphrey?

(NICHOLAS smiles broadly.)

MARGARET.

Nicholas,

Your smile is no pleasure to me.

NICHOLAS.

We fought for possession
of Alizon Eliot. What could have been more natural?
What he loves, I love. And if existence will
Molest a man with beauty, how can he help
Trying to impose on her the boundary
Of his two bare arms? . . .

(To bench C.)

O pandemonium,

What a fight, what a fight! It couldn't be more strenuous
Getting into heaven, or out again. And Humphrey
Went twinkling like Lucifer into the daffodils.
When Babylon fell there wasn't a better thump.

MARGARET.

Are you standing there letting your brother be rained on?
Haven't you any love for him?

NICHOLAS.

Yes, Mother,

But wet as well as dry.

MARGARET.

Can Richard carry him

Single-handed?

NICHOLAS.

Why can't he use both hands?
And how did I know it was going to rain?

(Exit U. R.)

MARGARET.

I would rather have to plait the tails of unbroken
Ponies than try to understand Nicholas.

(Bells start to ring. Heard off.)

Oh! It's bell-ringing practice. Their ding-dong rocks me,

17

Until I become the belfry, and makes bright blisters
All along my nerves.
(*Cuckoo starts singing.*)
                              Dear God, a cuckoo
    As well!
THOMAS. (*Down to level with desk.*)
                              By God, a cuckoo! Grief and God.
    A canting cuckoo, that laugh with no smile!
    A world unable to die sits on and on
    In spring sunshine, hatching egg after egg,
    Hoping against hope that out of one of them
    Will come the reason for it all; and always
    Out pops the arid chuckle and centuries
    Of cuckoo spit.
MARGARET.
                              I don't really think we need
    To let that worry us now.
    (*Bells again.* MARGARET *crosses to window and turns.*)
                              I don't know why you're waiting,
    Or who brought you, or whether I could even
    Begin to like you, but I know it would be agreeable
    If you left us.
    (*Goes* U. *to look out of window, then goes to chair* C.)
    There's enough going on already.
THOMAS. (*On step below desk.*)
    There is certainly enough going on. Madam, watch Hell come
    As a gleam into the eye of the wholesome cat
    When philip-sparrow flips his wing.
    I see a gleam of hell in *you*, madam.
    You understand those bells perfectly.
    I understand them too.
    What is it, that out there in the mellow street,
    The soft rain is raining on?
    It is only on the little sour grass, madam?
MARGARET.
    Out in the street? What could it be?
THOMAS.
                              It could be
    And it is, a witch hunt.

18

MARGARET.

Oh! . . . dear; another?

THOMAS.

Your innocence is on at such a rakish angle
It gives you quite an air of iniquity.
By the most naked of compassionate angels,
Hadn't you better answer that bell?
(Bells stop.)

With a mere
Clouding of your unoccupied eyes, madam.
Or a twitch of the neck; what better use can we put
Our faces to than to have them express kindness
When we're thinking of something else? Oh, be disturbed,
Be disturbed, madam, to the extent of a tut
And I will thank God for civilisation.
This is my last throw, my last poor gamble on the human
    heart.

(R. *of* MARGARET.)

MARGARET.

If I knew who you were
I would ask you to sit down. But while you're on
Your feet, would you be kind enough to see
How Humphrey's doing?

(Bells start again.)

THOMAS.

If we listened, we could hear
How the hunters, having washed the dinner things
Are now toiling up and down the blind alleys
Which they think are their immortal souls,
To scour themselves in the blood of a grandmother.
(Bells stop.)
They, of course, will feel all the better for it.
But she?
(Sits on bench R.)
Grandma? Is it possible
She may be wishing she had died yesterday,
That wicked sobbing old body of a woman?

MARGARET.

At the moment, as you know,
I'm trying hard to be patient with my sons,

19

. . . And you really mustn't expect me to be Christian
In two directions at once.

THOMAS.
                              What, after all,
Is a halo? It's one more thing to keep clean.
(*Going to window, looking out.*)
Richard and Nicholas
Have been trying to persuade the body to stand up.

ALIZON. (*Crosses, also looks from window.*)
Why, yes, he isn't dead. He's lying on his back
Picking the daffodils. And now they are trying
To lift him.
(*Looking slightly to off* U. R., *another part of garden.*)
                    I am sure that yellow and wet
Whistling is a blackbird. The hot sun
Is out again.

MARGARET. (*Comes to window.*)
                    Let me look over your shoulder.
They mustn't see me taking an interest.
Oh, the poor boy looks like a shock
Of bedraggled oats. . . . But you will see, Alizon,
What a nice boy he can be when he wears a clean shirt.
I more than once lost my heart to clean linen
When I was a young creature, even to linen
That hung on the hedges without a man inside it.
(*Coming back* C. *with* ALIZON.)
Do I seem composed, sufficiently placid and unmotherly?

ALIZON.
Altogether, except that your ear-ring
Trembles a little.

MARGARET.
                    It's always our touches of vanity
That manage to betray us.

THOMAS. (*Comes* C.)
When shall I see the Mayor?
I've had enough of this horror beating in the belfry.
Where is the Mayor?
(*Goes above desk and* NICHOLAS *carrying* HUMPHREY *from* U. R.
HUMPHREY *holds bunch of daffodils. They carry him across stage*
L.C.)

20

NICHOLAS.

    Here's Humphrey. Where would you like him?
(Bells stop.)

MARGARET.

    Humphrey, why do you have to be carried?

HUMPHREY.

                          My dear

Mother, I didn't knock myself down. Why
Should I pick myself up? . . . Daffodils
For my future wife.

(Holds out daffodils. MARGARET takes daffodils from him and hands them to ALIZON. MARGARET sits. RICHARD and NICHOLAS drop HUMPHREY L. C.)

NICHOLAS.

                       You slawsy poodle, you tike.

(Gets horoscope from rostrum.)

You crapulous puddering pipsqueak! Do I have to kill you
A second time? What about the stars?

(Waves horoscope at HUMPHREY.)

HUMPHREY. *(Takes horoscope, then hands it back.)*

                            All right;

What about the stars? They flicker and flicker,
Like Hell's light they flicker.

(Lies flat.)

NICHOLAS.

                      You dismal copralite!
Haven't they said that I shall have Alizon Eliot?

HUMPHREY.

    Astral delirium, dear Nick. Officially
    (Turning over, rises.)
Alizon is mine. What is official
Is incontestible. Without disrespect either
To you, Mother, or to my officially
    (Bows to each.)
Dear one, I shall lie down.
    (Starts to move L. Viol starts tuning offstage.)
    . . . Who is playing the viol?
(Sits on stool D. L.)

NICHOLAS.

    The Chaplain is tuning his fiddle to the bells.

21

It must be time for prayers.

MARGARET.
                                    It must be time for
Something. You're both transfigured with dirt!

THOMAS. (*Coming down.*)
        Where in thunder is the Mayor? Are you deaf to the baying
        Of those bib-and-tuckered bloodhounds out in the street?
        I want to be hanged.

NICHOLAS. (*To* HUMPHREY.)
                                    O blasterdom of injustice.
        You multiplication of double crossing!
        Alizon, who's going to marry you?

MARGARET.
        He deserves no answer.

RICHARD.
                                    Can you tell us, Alizon?

ALIZON.
        I'm not very used to things happening rapidly.
        The nuns, you see, were very quiet, especially
        In the afternoon. They say I shall marry Humphrey.

MARGARET.
        Certainly so. Now, Nicholas, go and get clean.

NICHOLAS. (*Crosses to* ALIZON.)
        She never shall.

THOMAS. (*On edge of rostrum.*)
                                    Will someone fetch the Mayor?
        Will no one make the least effort to let me
        Out of this world?

NICHOLAS.
                                    Let Humphrey go and officially
        Bury himself.

RICHARD.
        But what about . . . ?

NICHOLAS.
                                    She's not for him.

THOMAS. (C.)
                                    Let me get out!
        I'll find the Mayor myself wherever he may be having
        His pomposity of snobjoy snores,
        And you can go on with your psalm of love.

22

(*Goes to door* U. L., *opens it and is almost out as* TYSON *is about to enter.* THOMAS *bears* TYSON *and returns.*)

HUMPHREY.

    Who the hell's that?

RICHARD.

                The man about the gallows.

(NICHOLAS *to below desk. Enter* U. L. HEBBLE TYSON, *the Mayor, afflicted with office.*)

MARGARET. (*Rises.*)

    Now, here's your uncle. Do, for the sake of calm,
    Go and sweeten yourselves.

THOMAS. (*As* TYSON *crosses* C.)

                  Is this the man

    I long for?

(RICHARD *nods.*)

TYSON.

    Pest, who has stolen my handkerchief?

MARGARET.

    Use this one, Hebble.
    (*Gives him handkerchief. To* HUMPHREY *and* NICHOLAS.)

                  Go and get

    Under the pump.
(*Motions them off, picks up work-basket and puts it on bench.*
NICHOLAS *and* HUMPHREY *exit* U. L. THOMAS *moves* D. L.)

TYSON. (*Blowing his nose.*)

    Noses, noses.

THOMAS.

    Mr. Mayor, it's a joy to see you.
    You're about to become my gateway to eternal
    Rest.

TYSON.

    Dear sir, I haven't yet been notified
    Of your existence. As far as I'm concerned
    You don't exist. Therefore you are not entitled
    To any rest at all, eternal or temporary,
    And I would be obliged if you'd sit down.

MARGARET. (*Pushes* ALIZON *toward* TYSON.)

    Here is Alizon Eliot, Humphrey's bride
    To be.

THOMAS.

I have come to be hanged, do you hear?

TYSON.

Have you filled in the official application?
So this is the young lady?
(*Kisses* ALIZON.)

                              Very nice, very charming . . . in triplicate?
. . . And a very pretty dress.
Splendid material. I'm only sorry you had to come
On a troubled evening such as this promises
To be.

(MARGARET *takes* ALIZON *to bench* R. *Both sit.*)

The bells, you know. Richard, my boy,
What is it this importunate fellow wants?

RICHARD.

He says he wants to be hanged, sir.

TYSON.

                                        Out of the question.
It's the most immodest suggestion, which I know
Of no precedent for. Cannot be entertained.

(THOMAS *laughs.*)

I suspect an element of mockery
Directed at the ordinary decencies
Of life. . . . Tiresome catarrh. . . . A sense of humor
Incompatible with good citizenship—
And I wish you a good evening. Are we all
Assembled together for evening prayers?

(*As* TYSON *gets to desk* MARGARET *moves* C. *chair slightly up-stage. She sits.* RICHARD *gets prayer books from desk, gives one to* MARGARET *and one to* ALIZON, *who has put daffodils on work-basket on bench* R. RICHARD *puts bench in position for prayers,* U. *and* D. *stage on* R., *places prayer books on it, lifts work-basket up, and stands* R. *of bench.* ALIZON *brings stool from beside buttress, places it midway between bench and chair, and sits.*)

THOMAS. (*Rises and crosses to stand in front of desk.*)

                                        Oh no!
You can't postpone me. Since opening time I've been
Propped up at the bar of heaven and earth, between
The wall-eye of the moon and the brandy-cask of the sun,
Growling thick songs about jolly good fellows

24

In a mumping pub where the ceiling drips humanity,
Until I've drunk myself sick, and now, by Christ,
I mean to sleep it off in a stupor of dust
Till the morning after the day of judgment.
So put me on the waiting list for your gallows
With a note recommending preferential treatment.

TYSON.

Go away; you're an unappetising young man
With a tongue too big for your brains. I'm not at all sure
It would be amiss to suppose you to be a vagrant,
In which case an unfortunate experience
At the cart's tail. . . .

THOMAS.

Unacceptable.

Hanging or nothing.

TYSON.

Get this man away from here.

(RICHARD *goes to* THOMAS.)
Good gracious, do you imagine the gallows to be
A charitable institution? Very mad,
Wishes to draw attention to himself;
The brain a delicate mechanism; Almighty
God more precise than a clockmaker;
(*Kneels.*)
Grant us all a steady pendulum.
All say Amen.

ALL. (*Kneeling.*)
Amen.

THOMAS.

Listen! The wild music of the spheres;
Tick-tock.

RICHARD.

Come on; you've got to go.

(RICHARD *pushes* THOMAS *toward door* U. L. THOMAS *wrenches himself free and moves* D. L. *on steps.*)

THOMAS.

Does Justice with her sweet, impartial,
Devastating and deliberate sword
Never come to this place? Do you mean
There's no recognition given to murder here?

25

MARGARET.

    Murder?

TYSON.

                Now, what is it?

THOMAS. (*Crosses to* C. *of rostrum.*)

                      I'm not a fool.

I didn't suppose you would do me a favor for nothing.

No crime, no hanging; I quite understand the rules.

But I've made that all right. I managed to do-in

A rag-and-bone merchant at the bottom of Leapfrog Lane.

(ALIZON *gives a little cry, half-rises, then sits again.*)

TYSON (*Staring.*)

    Utterly unhinged.

MARGARET.

    Hebble, they're all

In the same April fit of exasperating nonsense.

Nicholas, too. He said he'd killed Humphrey,

But of course he hadn't. If he had I should have told you.

THOMAS.

    It was such a monotonous cry, that "Rags-and-bones!"

    (*Cuckoo is heard.*)

Like that damned cuckoo. It was more than time

He should see something of another world.

But poor old man, he wasn't anxious to go.

He picked on his rags and his bones as love

Picks upon hearts, he with an eye to profit

And love with an eye to pain.

RICHARD.

    Sanctus fumus!

TYSON.

    Get a complete denial of everything

He has said. I don't want to be bothered with you.

You don't belong to this village. I'm perfectly satisfied

He hasn't killed a man.

THOMAS.

                 I've killed two men,

If you want to be exact.

The other I thought scarcely worth mentioning;

A poor unprepossessing pimp with a birthmark.

(RICHARD *laughs.*)

26

He couldn't have had any affection for himself,
So I pulped him first and knocked him into the river
Where the water gives those girlish giggles, around
The ford, and held him under with my foot
Until he was safely in Abram's bosom, birthmark
And all.

(*Lifts his foot.*)

You see, it still isn't properly dry.

TYSON.

What a confounded thing! Who do people
Think they are, coming here without
Identity, and putting us to considerable
Trouble and expense to have them punished.
You don't deserve to be listened to.

THOMAS.

It's habit.

I've been unidentifiably
Floundering in Flanders for the past seven years.
Prising open ribs to let men go
On the indefinite leave that needs no pass.
And now all roads are uncommonly flat, and all hair
Stands on end.

(*Enter* NICHOLAS *through* R. *side of window, and stands on window-seat* R.)

NICHOLAS.

I'm sorry to interrupt,
But there's a witch to see you, Uncle.

TYSON.

To see me?

A witch to see me? I will not be the toy
Of irresponsible events. Is that clear
To you all?

NICHOLAS.

Yes, but she's here.

TYSON.

A witch to see me!

Do I have to tell you what to do with her?

NICHOLAS.

Don't tell me. My eyes do that only too well.
She's the one, of witches she's the one

27

Who most of all disturbs Hell's heart *Jimminy!*
How she must make Damnation sigh.
How she must make Torment be tormented
To have her to add to its torment! How the flames
Must burn to lay their tongues about her.
If evil has a soul it's here outside,
The dead-of-midnight flower, Satan's latest
Button-hole. Shall I ask her in?

THOMAS. (*Looking out of window.*)

                                She's young,
Oh, God, she's young.

TYSON.

                       I stare at you, Nicholas,
With no word of condemnation. I stare
Astonished at your behavior.

MARGARET. (*At study door* R.)

                           Ask her in?
In here? Nicholas . . .

THOMAS.

                       Nicholas! Expose
The backside of immorality before ladies?
Your mother would never be able to get the smell
Of sulphur out of the curtains.

(*Stands on window-seat* L.)

NICHOLAS.

                     She's the glorious
Undercoat of this painted world . . .

(JENNET JOURDEMAYNE *runs across back of window to* R.
and in through door U. R. *She is breathless as she leans
against buttress.*)

                           . . . you see;
It comes through, however much of our whiteness
We paint over it.

TYSON. (*Rising.*)
What is the meaning of this?

(*Picks up Bible.*)
What is the meaning of this?

(*During next speeches* RICHARD *moves slowly to* L. *of lectern,
only slightly downstage from where he is.*)

28

THOMAS.

                                That's the most relevant
Question in the world.

JENNET.

                                 Will someone say
Come in? And understand I don't every day
Break in on the quiet circle of a family
At prayers. Not quite so unceremoniously,
Or so shamefully near a flood of tears.
(*Crosses down to stool* R. C. *and sits.*)
Or looking as unruly as I surely do. Will you
Forgive me?

TYSON.

                      You'll find I can't be disarmed
With pretty talk, young woman. You have no business
At all in this house.

JENNET. (*Rises to behind chair* C.)

                        Do you know how many walls
There are between the garden of the Magpie,
Past Lazer's field, Slink Alley and Poorsoul Pond
To the gate of your paddock?

TYSON.

                          I'm not to be seduced.
I'm not attending.
(*Sits.*)

JENNET.

                      Eight. I've come over them all.

MARGARET.

How could she have done?

THOMAS.

                      Her broomstick's in the hall.

MARGARET.

Come over to this side of the room, Nicholas.

NICHOLAS.

Don't worry, Mother, I have my fingers crossed.

TYSON.

Never before in the whole term of my office
Have I met such an extraordinary ignorance
Of what is permitted . . .

29

JENNET. (*Crosses to desk.*)

Indeed I was ignorant
They were hooting and howling for me, as though echoes
Could kill me. So I took to my toes. Thank God
I only passed one small girl in a shady
Ditch telling the beads of her daisy chain.
And a sad rumpled idiot-boy
Who smiled at me. They say I have turned a man
Into a dog.

(ALIZON *joins* MARGARET D. R.)

TYSON. (*Writing.*)

This will all be gone into
At the proper time. . . .

JENNET.

But it isn't a dog at all.
It's a bitch; an appealing, rueful, brindle bitch
With many fleas. Are you a gentleman
Full of ripe, friendly wisdom?

TYSON.

This
Will all be gone into at the proper . . .

JENNET.

If so
I will sit at your feet. I will sit anyway;
I'm tired. Eight walls are enough.

(*Sits edge of rostrum below desk.*)

MARGARET.

What are we to do?
I can almost feel the rustling in of some
Kind of enchantment already.

TYSON. (*Rises.*)

She will have
To be put in charge.

ALIZON.

Oh, must she, must she?

THOMAS.

He can see she's a girl of property,
And the property goes to the town if she's a witch;
She couldn't have been more timely.

30

NICHOLAS.

Curious, crooked

Beauty of the earth. Fascinating.

TYSON. (*To* JENNET.)

Get up at once, you undisciplined girl. Have you never
Heard of law and order?

NICHOLAS. (*Rises, places chair* C. *for* JENNET.)

Won't you use

This chair?

(R. *of chair.*)

JENNET. (*Rises, crosses and sits in chair.*)

Thank you. Oh, this is the reasonable

World again! I promise not to leave behind me
Little flymarks of black magic, or any familiars
Such as mice or beetles, which might preach
Demonology in your skirting board.

(THOMAS *moves downstage to* JENNET'S L. MARGARET *motions* NICHOLAS *to leave* JENNET. NICHOLAS *sits stool* R. C.
RICHARD *sits on steps leading to doors* U. L. D. L.)

I have wiped my shoes so that I shouldn't bring in
The soft Egyptian sand which drifts at night,
They tell me, into the corners of my house
And then with the approach of naked morning
Flies into the fire like a shadow of goldfinches.
The tales unbelievable, the wild
Tales they tell!

TYSON.

This will be discussed

At the proper time . . .

THOMAS. (*Moves quickly to desk and bangs on it.*)

When we have finished talking

About my murders.

MARGARET. (*Crosses to* U. L. *of* JENNET'S *chair.* TYSON *moves
down to* C. *on step.*)

O peaceful and placid heaven,

Are they both asking to be punished? Has death
Become the fashionable way to live?
Nothing would surprise me in their generation.

JENNET.

Asking to be punished? why no, I have come

Here to have the protection of your laughter.
They accuse me of such a brainstorm of absurdities
That all my fear dissolves in the humor of it.
If I could perform what they say I *can* perform
I could have got safely away from here
As fast as you bat an eyelid.

TYSON.

Oh indeed;

Could you indeed?

JENNET.

They say I have only
To crack a twig, and over the springtime weathercocks
Cloudburst, hail and gale, whatever you will
Come leaping fury-foremost.

(THOMAS *whistles.*)

TYSON. (*Between* JENNET *and* MARGARET *on step.*)

The report
May be exaggerated, of course, but where there's smoke . . .

JENNET.

They also say that I bring back the past;
For instance, Helen comes
Brushing the maggots from her eyes,
And, clearing her throat of several thousand years
She says "I loved . . ."; but cannot any longer
Remember names. Sad Helen.

(TYSON *crosses* R. *of* JENNET. RICHARD *kneels* D. L. NICHOLAS *lies on floor down-stage of* JENNET.)

Or Alexander, wearing
His imperial cobwebs and breastplate of shining worms
Wakens and looks for his glasses, to find the empire
Which he knows he put beside his bed.

(THOMAS *laughs.*)

TYSON. (*Sits stool* R. C.)

Whatever you say will be taken down in evidence
Against you; am I making myself clear?

(MARGARET *crosses to* R. *of chair* C.)

JENNET.

They tell one tale that once, when the moon
Was gibbous and in a high dazed state
Of nimbus love, I shook a jonquil's dew

32

On to a pearl, and let a cricket chirp
Three times, thinking of pale Peter;
(*Rises.*)
And there Titania was, vexed by a cloud
Of pollen, using the sting of a bee to clean
Her nails, and singing, as drearily as a gnat,
'Why try to keep clean?'
(*Moves up to* R. *window seat.*)

THOMAS.
    'The earth is all of earth' . . .
        So sang the queen;
        So the queen sung,
Crumbling her crownet into clods of dung.
(*Sits on rostrum.*)

JENNET.
    You heard her too, Captain? Bravo! Is that
A world you've got there, hidden under your hat?

THOMAS.
    Bedlam, ma'am, and the battlefield
Uncle Adam died on.
    (JENNET *to behind chair* C.)
                He was shot
To bits with the core of an apple
Which some fool of a serpent in the artillery
Had shoved into God's cannon.

TYSON. (*Moves to* C. *step round* L. *of chair* C.)
                    That's enough!
Terrible frivolity, terrible blasphemy,
Awful unorthodoxy. I can't understand
Anything that's being said. Fetch a constable.
The woman's tongue clearly knows the flavor
Of *spiritu maligno*. The man must be
Drummed out of the town.
(MARGARET *sits stool* R. C.)

THOMAS.
                Oh, *must he be?*

RICHARD. (*On step* D. L.)
    Are you certain, sir? The constable? The lady
Was laughing. She laughed at the very idea
Of being a witch, sir.

33

TYSON.

Yes, just it, just it.
Giving us a rigmarole of her dreams;
Probably dreams; but intentionally
Recollected, intentionally consented to,
Intentionally delighted in. And so
As dangerous as the act. Fetch the constable.

(*Moves* D. L.)

NICHOLAS.

Sad, how things always are. We get one gulp
Of dubious air from our hellmost origins
And we have to bung up the draught with a constable.
It's a terribly decontaminating life.

TYSON.

I'll not have any frivolity. The town
Goes in terror.

MARGARET.

Sin is so inconvenient.

ALIZON. (*Goes to* MARGARET.)

She is lovely. She is certain to be good.

(JENNET *rises, facing* U. S.)

TYSON. (*Goes above* NICHOLAS *to face* RICHARD.)

I have told you twice, Richard, what to do.
Are you going about it?

RICHARD.

No, sir. Not yet.

(THOMAS *laughs.*)

TYSON. (*To* RICHARD.)

Did you speak to me? Now be careful how you answer.

JENNET. (*Up to* R. *of desk.*)

Can you be serious? I am Jennet Jourdemayne
And I believe in the human mind. Why play with me
And make me afraid of you, as you did for a moment,
I confess it.

(CROWD *is heard off-stage* R. NICHOLAS *goes to window,*
RICHARD *to lectern,* MARGARET *and* ALIZON *to window.* ALIZON
sits R. *window-seat.* JENNET *sits below desk.* TYSON *backs*
D. L. *on step.* THOMAS *goes to buttress, then goes* U. R.)

You can't believe . . . oh, surely not,
When the centuries of the world are piled so high . . .

You'll not believe what in their innocence
Those old credulous children in the street
Imagine of me.

THOMAS.

Innocence! Dear girl!

TYSON. (*Crossing* C.)

Will be

Gone into at the proper time. Disturbing
The peace. In every way. Have to arrest you.

JENNET. (*With back to wall by lectern.*)

No!

(THOMAS *moves across stage to* TYSON *during speech.* NICHOLAS
goes above desk.)

THOMAS.

You bubble-mouthing, fog-blathering,
Chin-chuntering, chap-flapping, liturgical,
Turgidical, base old man! What about my murders?

(TYSON *sits chair* C., THOMAS L. *of him.* MARGARET *moves to
buttress.*)

And what goes round in *your* head,
What funny little murders and fornications
Chatting up and down in three-four time
Afraid to come out? What bliss to sin by proxy
And do penance by way of someone else!
But we'll not talk about you. It will make the outlook
So dark. Neither about this exquisitely
Mad young woman. Nor about this congenital
Generator, your nephew there;
Nor about anyone but me. I'm due
To be hanged.

(TYSON *rises, goes round* L. *of chair up to desk.* THOMAS
follows to U. C.)

Good Lord, aren't two murders enough
To win me the medals of damnation? Must I put
Half a dozen children on a spit
And toast them at the flame that comes out of my mouth?

(NICHOLAS *moves* L. *to allow* TYSON *to get to desk.*)

You let the fairies fox you while the devil
Does you. Concentrate on me.

35

TYSON. (*At desk.*)

                              I'll not
Have it . . . I'll . . . I'll . . . I'll . . .
(*Sits.*)
THOMAS. (R. *of desk.*)

                              Power of Job!
Must I wait for a stammer? Your life, sir, is propelled
By a dream of the fear of having nightmares; your love
By the fear of your single self; your world's history
The fear of a possible leap by a possible antagonist
Out of a possible shadow, or a not improbable
Skeleton out of your dead-certain cupboard.
But here am I, the true phenomenon
Of acknowledged guilt, steaming with the blood
Of the pimp and the rag-and-bone man, crime
Transparent. What the hell are we waiting for?
TYSON.
Will you attend to me? Will you be silent?
JENNET. (*A step forward.*)
Are you doing this to save me?
THOMAS.   '

                         You flatter my powers,
My sweet, you're too much a woman. But if you wish
You can go down to the dinner of damnation
On my arm.
JENNET.

              I dine elsewhere.
(*Moves* D. L. *to steps.*)
TYSON.

                      Am I invisible?
Am I inaudible? Do I merely festoon
The room with my presence? Richard, wretched boy,
If you don't wish to incur considerable punishment
Do yourself the kindness to fetch the constable.
I don't care for these unexpurgated persons.
I shall lose my patience.
(JENNET *sits on steps* D. L.)
MARGARET. (U. C.)

                   I shall lose my faith
In the good breeding of providence. Wouldn't this happen

36

Now: today; within an hour or two
Of everyone coming to congratulate
Humphrey and Alizon. Arrangements were made
A month ago, long before this gentleman's
Murders were even thought of.

(NICHOLAS *goes to window when noise is heard outside, and*
THOMAS *goes to door* U. R.)

TYSON.

                                    They don't exist,

I say . . .

(*Enter* HUMPHREY *from* U. L.)

HUMPHREY.

                        Uncle, there's a sizeable rumpus,
Without exaggeration a how-do-you-do
Taking place in the street. I thought you should know.

(MARGARET *takes* ALIZON *to below buttress* R.)

TYSON.

Rumpus?

(NICHOLAS *moves to* R. *of desk.*)

HUMPHREY. (*Above desk.*)

                        Perhaps rumpus isn't the word.
A minor kind of bloody revolution.

(THOMAS *laughs and moves* D. R. *to* L. *of bench.*)

It's this damned rascal, this half-pay half-wit.
I should say he's certifiable. It seems
He's been spreading all around the town some tale
About drowning a pimp and murdering Old Skipps,
The rag-and-bone man.

THOMAS.

                        Ah, Old Skipps, Old Skipps,
What a surplus of bones you'll have where you've gone to
    now!

JENNET. (*Rises.*)

Old Skipps? But he's the man . . .

TYSON.

                                    Will you both be silent?
I won't have every Tom, Dick and Harry
Laying information against himself before
He's got written authority from me.

(*Bangs desk.* JENNET *sits on step* D. L.)

HUMPHREY.

Quite right.
As it is the town is hell's delight. They've looked
For the drowned pimp and they've looked for Skipps,
And they've looked in the places where he says he left them,
And they can't find either.

NICHOLAS.

Can't find either?

HUMPHREY.

Can't find either.

MARGARET. (*Taking* ALIZON *to bench* R.)
Of course they can't. When he first
Mentioned murders I knew he had got hold
Of a quite wrong end of the stick.

HUMPHREY. (*Still behind desk, points at* THOMAS.)
They say he's the Devil.

MARGARET.

I can imagine who started *that* story.

HUMPHREY.

But are we so sure he isn't? Outside in the street
They're convinced he's the Devil. And none of us ever having
Seen the Devil, how can we know? They say
He killed the old men and spirited them into the Limbo.
We can't search there. I don't even know where it is.

THOMAS. (*Having made up his mind to play the Devil.*)
Sir, it's between me and the deep blue sea.
The wind of conscience blows straight from its plains.

HUMPHREY.

Shut up!

(THOMAS *rises.*)
If you're the Devil I beg your pardon.

(HUMPHREY *goes to rostrum below desk, speaks upstage to*
TYSON. THOMAS *goes* U. C.)
They also have the idea
He's got a girl in his toils, a witch called . . .

MARGARET.

Sssh!

(NICHOLAS *points to* JENNET.)
Jennet.
I am she.

38

HUMPHREY.
    God.
(*Turns and comes off rostrum. Whistles.* MARGARET *sits stool* R. C.)
TYSON.
            Well, Humphrey, well?
        Is that the end of your information?
NICHOLAS.
                            Humphrey,
        Have you spoken to your little future wife
        Lately?
THOMAS. (*Moving* U. R.)
            Tinder, easy tinder.
HUMPHREY. (*Moving toward* JENNET.)
                    In fact . . .
    In fact . . .
(THOMAS *sits* R. *window-seat.*)
NICHOLAS. (*Pushes* HUMPHREY *upstage to rostrum, fighting with him.*)
        In fact it's all a bloody revolution.
(*Both sit,* NICHOLAS R., HUMPHREY L.)
TYSON.
        I'm being played with, I'm sure of it. Something tells me
        There's irresponsibility somewhere. Richard.
        (RICHARD *crosses and stands in front of desk facing* TYSON.)
        You'll not get out of this lightly. Where is the constable?
        Why isn't he standing before me?
RICHARD.
                        I see
        No need for the constable, sir.
TYSON.
                        No need? No need?
(CHAPLAIN *enters* U. R., *carrying his viol and music.*)
CHAPLAIN. (*Speaking as he enters and coming to chair* C.)
        I am late for prayers, I know; I know you think me
        A broken reed and my instrument, too, my better half.
        You lacked it, I'm afraid. But life has such
        Diversity, I sometimes remarkably lose
        Eternity in the passing moment.
        (TYSON *rises, motions all to rise for prayers.* NICHOLAS *and*

HUMPHREY *cross to bench* R. JENNET *rises.* CHAPLAIN *crosses to* R. *of lectern, arranges music, and sits on edge of rostrum.*)

                                            Just now
In the street there's a certain boisterous interest
In a spiritual matter. They say . . .

(*Sees* JENNET.)

TYSON.

                                    I know what they say.

CHAPLAIN.

Ah, yes, you know. Sin, as well as God,
Moves in a most mysterious way.

(*All are now in their positions for prayers.* MARGARET *in chair* C. ALIZON *on stool* R. C. RICHARD *behind bench* R. HUMPHREY *and* NICHOLAS *sitting on bench* R. TYSON *motions them to stand, starts to count for opening hymn. Before they can start,* CHAPLAIN *speaks.*)

                                    It's hard to imagine
Why the poor girl should turn Skipps into a dog.

NICHOLAS. (*Crossing to* R. *of chair* C.)

Skipps? Skipps into a dog?

HUMPHREY. (*Crossing to behind* NICHOLAS.)

                                    But Skipps . . .

THOMAS. (*Rises, goes to* C. *of step.*)

Skipps trundles in another place, calling
His raga-boa in gutters without end.
Transfigured by the spatial light
Of Gargage Indestructible. And I
Ought to know since I sent him there. A dog?
Come, come, don't let's be fanciful.

(*Goes to stool* D. L. *and sits.*)

TYSON.

They say one thing, and another thing, and both at once.
I don't know. It will all have to be gone into
At the proper time . . .

(*Tries to start hymn.*)

HUMPHREY. (*On* C. *step of rostrum.*)

But this is a contradiction. . . .

CHAPLAIN. (*Rises and moves towards* HUMPHREY.)

Ah, isn't that life all over!

(*Looks at* THOMAS.)

40

The young assassin?

(THOMAS *shakes hands with him.* ALIZON, MARGARET *and*
TYSON *sit.* NICHOLAS *sits on rostrum step* R. *of* MARGARET.)

                    If he is the doer of the damage,
Can it be she also? My flock are employing
Fisticuffs over this very question.

(*Shakes* JENNET'S *hand.*)

HUMPHREY. (*Crossing* D. C. *on step.*)

    But if he could be the Devil . . .

THOMAS. (*Rises.*)

    Good boy.

    (*Crosses upstage* C. *on rostrum.*)

            Shall I set
Your minds at rest and give you proof? Come here.

(HUMPHREY *crosses to* THOMAS, *on his* L. THOMAS *takes prayer
book out of his hand, whispers in his ear, gives book back to him.*
HUMPHREY *backs to above desk.*)

HUMPHREY.

    That's not funny.

THOMAS.

              Not funny for the goats.

HUMPHREY.

    I've heard it before. He says the Day of Judgment
Is fixed for tonight.

(NICHOLAS *rises by buttress,* ALIZON R. *of stool.*)

MARGARET.

    Oh, no. I have always been sure
That when it comes it will come in autumn.
Heaven, I am quite sure, wouldn't disappoint
The bulbs.

(JENNET *sits steps* D. L.)

THOMAS.

             Consider: vastiness lusted, Mother;
A huge heaving desire, overwhelming solitude,
And the mountain belly of time labored
And brought forth man, the mouse. The spheres churned on,
Hoping to charm our ears
With sufficient organ music, sadly sent out
On the wrong wave of sound; but still they roll

Fabulous and fine, a roundabout
Of doomed and golden notes. And on beyond,
Profound with thunder of oceanic power,
Lie the morose dynamics of our dumb friend
Jehovah.

(*Looks at* CHAPLAIN. *Rises, to* U. C.)

Why should these omnipotent bombinations
Go on with the deadly human anecdote, which
From the first was never more than remotely funny?
No; the time has come for tombs to tip
Their refuse: for the involving ivy, the briar,
The convolutions of convolvulous,
To disentangle and make way
For the last great ascendancy of dust,
Sucked into judgment by a cosmic yawn
Of boredom. The Last Trump
Is timed for twenty-two forty hours precisely.

TYSON.

This will all be gone into at the proper . . .

THOMAS. (*Turning to* TYSON.)

                                 Time

Will soon be most improper. Why not hang me
Before it's too late?

MARGARET. (*Looks at* THOMAS, *rises and crosses* L.)

I shall go and change my dress;
Then I shall both be ready for our guests
And whatever else may come upon the world.

(*Exit* U. L. *door.*)

HUMPHREY.

I'm sure he's mad.

(ALIZON *rises, goes to below buttress.* NICHOLAS *goes to desk.*
CHAPLAIN *moves to below desk.* THOMAS *goes to chair* C., *moves
it slightly* R., *then leans against it, back to audience.*)

CHAPLAIN.

               And his information, of course,
Is in opposition to what is plainly told
In the Scriptures: that the hour will come . . .

NICHOLAS.

                           Do you think
He means it? I've an idea he's up to something
None of us knows about, not one of us.

ALIZON. (*Who has found her way to* RICHARD.)

Quiet Richard, son of nobody.

RICHARD.

It isn't always like this, I promise it isn't.

(JENNET *crosses* C., *looks at* THOMAS, *then to* C. *of rostrum, facing desk.*)

JENNET.

May I, Jennet Jourdemayne, the daughter
Of a man who believed the universe to be governed
By certain laws, be allowed to speak?
Here is such a storm of superstition
And humbug and curious passions, where will you start
To look for the truth? Am I in fact
An enchantress bemused into collaboration
With the enemy of man? Is this the enemy,
This eccentric young gentleman never seen by me
Before? I say I am not. He says perhaps
He is. You say I am. You say he is not.
And now the eccentric young gentleman threatens us all
With imminent cataclysm. If, as a living creature,
I wish in all good faith to continue living,
Where do you suggest I should lodge my application?

TYSON.

That is perfectly clear. You are both under arrest.

THOMAS.

Into Pandora's box with all the ills.
But not if that little Hell-cat Hope's
Already in possession. I've hoped enough.
I gave the best years of my life to that girl,
But I'm walking out with Damnation now, and she's
A flame that's got finality.

(TYSON, CHAPLAIN, HUMPHREY *and* NICHOLAS *confer at desk.*)

JENNET. (*To* THOMAS' L., *kneels.*)

Do you want no hope for me either? No compassion
To lift suspicion off me?

THOMAS.

                    Lift? Compassion
Has a rupture, lady. To hell with lifting.

(NICHOLAS *goes* C., *facing desk.* CHAPLAIN *to front of desk. Noise from group round desk.*)

43

JENNET. (*Going toward desk.*)

Listen, please listen to me.

THOMAS.

Let the world

Go, lady; it isn't worth the candle.

TYSON. (*Hands bunch of keys to* RICHARD, *who takes* JENNET
D. L.)

Richard, take her away, down to the cellars.

THOMAS. (*Rises to above chair* C., *as they go to cellar door* L.)

You see, he has the key

To every perplexity. Kiss your illusions

For me before they go.

JENNET. (*Turning back from cellar door* L.)

But what will happen?

THOMAS.

That's something even old Nosedrip doesn't know!

(RICHARD *and* JENNET *exit* L. *door.*)

Mr. Mayor, hang me for pity's sake,

For God's sake hang me, before I love that woman!

(*Starts to move* D. L. *as curtain falls.*)

CURTAIN

44

ACT II

SCENE: *The same room.*

TIME: *About an hour later.*

When curtain is up, CHAPLAIN *is sleeping in chair on* R.
*of fire. The tongs are under his feet. After rise of
curtain* TAPPERCOOM *enters from cellar door* L., *carrying
lantern. He crosses to below desk where he places lantern, blowing it out. He is followed by* TYSON. *He goes
to below desk on* TAPPERCOOM'S L.)

TAPPERCOOM.

Well, it's poss-ss-ible, it's poss-ss-ible.
I *may* have been putting the Devil to the torture.
But can you smell scorching? . . . not a singe
For my sins . . .

(TYSON *points out burnt spot on* TAPPERCOOM'S *sleeve, looks
up at him questioningly.)*

that's from yesterday: I leaned
Across a candle. For all practical purposes
I feel as unblasted as on the day I was born.
(Moves U. *to desk, sits.)*
And God knows I'm a target. Cupid scarcely
Needs to aim, and no devil can miss me.

TYSON.

But his action may be delayed. We really must
Feel our way. We don't want to put ourselves wrong
With anything as positive as evil.

TAPPERCOOM.

We have put him to the merest thumb-screw, Tyson,
Courteously and impartially, the purest
Cajolery to coax him to deny
Those cock-and-bull murders for which there isn't a scrap
Of evidence.

(Looks at paper.)

TYSON. *(Looks at his papers.)*

Ah; ah. And how does he take it?
He hasn't denied them?

45

TAPPERCOOM. (*Pointing at each item.*)

On the contrary.

He says he has also committed petty larceny,

Abaction, peculation and incendiarism.

As for the woman Jourdemayne . . .

TYSON.

Ah, yes,

Jourdemayne. What are we to make of her?

Wealthy, they tell me. But on the other hand

Quite affectingly handsome. Sad, you know,

We see where the eye cannot come, eh, Tappercoom?

And all's not glorious within; no use

Saying it is. . . . I had a handkerchief.

(*Finds it* D. R. *of bench among his papers.*)

Ah yes, buried amongst all this evidence.

(*Blows his nose.*)

TAPPERCOOM.

Now no poetics, Tyson. Blow your nose

And avoid lechery. Keep your eye on the evidence

Against her; there's plenty of it there.

(TYSON *sits on stool* C.)

Religion

Has made an honest woman of the supernatural

And we won't have it kicking over the traces again.

Will we, Chaplain? . . . In the Land of Nod.

Admirable man.

(*Sits on bench* L.)

TYSON.

Humanity,

That's all, Tappercoom; it's perfectly proper.

No one is going to let it interfere

With anything serious. I use it with the greatest

Discretion, I assure you.—Has she confessed?

TAPPERCOOM. (*Looks toward cellar door* L.)

Not at all. Though we administer persuasion

With the greatest patience,

(*Looks at* TYSON.)

she admits nothing.

(*Looks* D. L.)

And the man

46

Won't stop admitting. It really makes one lose
All faith in human nature.

(*Enter* MARGARET *from upstairs* L., U. L. *door, without her placidity.*)

MARGARET. (*On steps* L.)

Who has the tongs?
The tongs, Hebble dear, the tongs! Sweet
(*Comes* C.)
Elijah, we shall all go up in flames!

TYSON.

Flames!
(*Rises and clutches* TAPPERCOOM, *dropping papers.*)
Did you hear that, Tappercoom? Flames!
My sister said flames!

(TAPPERCOOM *looks at* MARGARET.)

MARGARET.

A log the size of a cheese
Has fallen off my fire! Well, where are they?
Oh, what men of action!
(*Crosses* C.)
Tongs, I said!
(*Crosses below bench and fire to* CHAPLAIN.)
Chaplain.
They're under your feet!
(CHAPLAIN *wakens, exclaims, and* MARGARET *picks up tongs and moves below bench to stairs* L.)
Very simple you'd look
As a pile of ashes.

(*Exit* U. L.)

TYSON.

Oh, I beg your pardon,
Tappercoom. A blazing log.
(*Rising, picking up papers.*)

CHAPLAIN. (*Rises and picks up last piece of paper.*)
Would there be something
I could do? I was asleep, you know.
(*Sits again.*)

TYSON. (*Takes paper from* CHAPLAIN, *sits on stool* C.)
All this evidence from the witchfinder . . .

47

TAPPERCOOM.

>   The advent of a woman cannot be
> Too gradual. I am not a nervous man,
> But I like to be predisposed to an order of events.

CHAPLAIN.

>   It was very interesting: I was dreaming I stood
> On Jacob's ladder, waiting for the gates to open.
> And the ladder was made entirely of diminished sevenths.
> I was surprised but not put out. Nothing
> Is altogether what we suppose it to be.

TAPPERCOOM.

>   As for the Day of Judgment, we can be sure
> It's not due yet. What are we told the world
> Will be like? "Boasters, blasphemers, without natural
> (*Hymn singing starts off stage* L.)
> Affection, traitors, trucebreakers," and the rest of it.
> Come, we've still a lot of backsliding ahead of us.

(*Pats* TYSON. *Crowd mixes in with singing.*)

TYSON

>   Are you uneasy, Tappercoom?

TAPPERCOOM.

>   No, Tyson.
>   The whole thing's a lot of amphigourious
> Stultiloquential fiddle-faddle!

(*Noise of crowd and singing increases. Re-enter* MARGARET, *down stairs* U. L. *Stands on foot of steps.*)

MARGARET.

>   Hebble!

TAPPERCOOM.

>   For God's sake!

TYSON.

>   What is it now? What is it?

MARGARET. (*Crosses up to window* C. TYSON *to her* L. TAPPERCOOM *to buttress.*)

>   The street's gone mad. They've seen a shooting star.

TYSON.

>   They? Who? What of it?

MARGARET.

>   I'm sure I'm sorry,
> But the number of people gone mad in the street

48

Is particularly excessive.
(*Cross* D. C. *on rostrum in front of* TYSON.)
                              They were shaking
Our gate, and knocking off each other's hats.
(TYSON *goes up to window* C. *on* MARGARET'S R., *leans out.*)
And six fights simultaneously,
(*Shouts off. A piece of turf is thrown at window from stage*
L., *hitting* TYSON *on the face. He backs downstage* C. *on*
rostrum. MARGARET *wipes his eye. He says "Oh!" She says*
"Ah!" To L. *of* TYSON.)
                              and some
Were singing psalm a hundred and forty . . . I think
It's a hundred and forty . . . and the rest of them shouting
"The Devil's in there?" (pointing at this house.)
"Safety from Satan!" and "Where's the woman? Where's
The witch? Send her out!" and using words
That are only fit for the Bible. And I'm sure
There was blood in the gutter from somebody's head
Or else it was the sunset in a puddle,
But Jobby Pinnock was prising up cobblestones,
Roaring like the north wind, and you know
What he is in church when he starts on the responses.
And that old Habakkuk Brown using our wall
As it was never meant to be used. And then
They saw a star fall over our roof somewhere
And followed its course with a downrush of whistling
And Ohs and Ahs and groans and screams; and Jobby
Pinnock dropped a stone on his own foot
And roared "Almighty God, it's a sign!" and some
Went down on their knees and others fell over them
(*Shouts off. Crowd in street gets louder again and almost at*
once the singing re-starts. MARGARET *goes up to window.*
TYSON *and* TAPPERCOOM *to window and look out.* CHAPLAIN
to study door R.)
And they've started to fight again, and the hundred and
          fortieth
Psalm has begun again louder and faster than ever.
(*Pushes* TYSON *over* L.)
Hebble dear, isn't it time they went home?

(CHAPLAIN *goes to window.*)
TYSON. (L.)

All right, all right, all right. Now why
Can't people mind their own business!
(*Crowd is silenced. Singing stops.* NICHOLAS' *voice can be
heard speaking to crowd.* TYSON *crosses down to bench.*)
This shooting star
Has got nothing to do with us, I am quite happy
In my mind about that. It probably went past,
Perfectly preoccupied with some astral anxiety or other
Without giving us a second thought. Eh, Tappercoom?
(TAPPERCOOM *comes* D. C. TYSON *sits on bench* R.)
One of those quaint astrological holus-boluses,
Quite all right.

TAPPERCOOM.

Quite. An excess of phlegm
In the solar system. It's on its way
To a heavenly spittoon. How is that,
How is that? On its way . . .

TYSON.

I consider it unwise
To tempt providence with humor, Tappercoom.

MARGARET.

And on the one evening when we expect company!
What company is going to venture to get here
Through all that heathen hullabaloo in the road?
Except the glorious company of the Apostles,
And we haven't enough glasses for all that number.

(*During next speech* CHAPLAIN *comes slowly down-stage between*
MARGARET *and* TAPPERCOOM.)

TAPPERCOOM.

Doomsday or not, we must keep our integrity.
We cannot set up dangerous precedents
Of speed. We shall sincerely hope, of course,
That Doomsday will refrain from precipitous action,
But the way we have gone must be the way we arrive.

CHAPLAIN.

I wish I were a thinking man very much.
Of course I feel a good deal, but that's no help to you.

50

(During next speech he moves over to chair R., glancing round for his viol.)

TYSON.

    I'm not bewildered, I assure you I'm not
    Bewildered. As a matter of fact a plan
    Is almost certainly forming itself in my head
    At this very moment. It may even be adequate.

CHAPLAIN. *(Preparing to sit on his chair where he has placed viol.)*

    Where did I put my better half? I laid it
    Aside.

    (MARGARET screams and points to chair. CHAPLAIN sees viol, picks it up.)

        Angel! I could take it down to the gate and perhaps
    Disperse them with a skirmish or two of the bow.
    Orpheus, you know, was very successful in that way,
    But of course I haven't his talent, not nearly his talent.

(Sits chair R.)

TYSON. *(Crosses D. L.)*

    If you would allow me to follow my train of thought . . .

(TAPPERCOOM rises. TYSON sits D. L. stool.)

TAPPERCOOM.

    It's my belief the woman Jourdemayne
    Got hold of the male prisoner by unlawful
    Supernatural soliciting.
    And bewitched him into a confession of murder
    To draw attention away from herself.
                    But the more
    We coax him to withdraw his confession, the more
    Crimes he confesses to.

CHAPLAIN.

                  I know I am not
    A practical person; legal matters and so forth
    Are Greek to me; except of course
    That I understand Greek.

    (Rises.)

              And what may seem nonsensical
    To men of affairs like yourselves might not seem so
    To me, since everything astonishes me,
    Myself most of all. When I think of myself
    I can scarcely believe my senses. But there it is,

All my friends tell me I actually exist
And by an act of faith I have come to believe them.
But this fellow who is being such a trouble to us
He, on the contrary, is so convinced
He *is* that he wishes he were not. Now why
Should that be?

TAPPERCOOM.

                        I believe you mean to tell us,
Chaplain.

MARGARET.

                   I might as well sit down, for all
The good standing up does.

CHAPLAIN.

                            I imagine
He finds the world not entirely salubrious.
If he cannot be stayed with flagons, or comforted
With apples . . . I quote of course . . . or the light, the
    ocean,
The everchanging . . . I mean and stars, extraordinary
How many, or some instrument or other . . . I am afraid
I appear rhapsodical—but perhaps the addition
Of your thumbscrew will not succeed, either.
(*Steps towards* TAPPERCOOM.)

                             The point
I am attempting to make is this one: he might be wooed
From his aptitude for death by being happier;
And what I was going to suggest, quite irresponsibly,
Is that he might be invited to partake
(*Sits stool.*)
Of our festivities this evening.
(*Pause.*)

                         No,
I see it astonishes you.

MARGARET.

    Do you mean ask him . . . ?
(*Turns to* TYSON.)

TYSON. (*Rises and crosses to above bench.*)

    I have heard very little of what you have said, Chaplain,
Being concerned as I am with a certain Thought,
But am I to believe that you recommend our inviting

52

This undesirable character to rub shoulders
With my sister?

CHAPLAIN.

Ah; rubbing shoulders. I hadn't exactly
Anticipated that.

(TYSON *goes back to stool* L. *and sits.*)
It was really in relation to the soul
That the possibility crossed my mind.

TAPPERCOOM.

As a criminal the man's a liability.
I doubt very much if he could supply a farthing
Towards the cost of his execution. So
You suggest, Chaplain, we let him bibulate
From glass to glass this evening, help him to
A denial of his guilt and get him off our hands
Before daybreak gets the town on its feet again?

MARGARET.

I wish I could like the look of the immediate future,
But I don't.

TYSON. (*Crosses to* L. *of bench.*)
I'm glad to tell you
An idea has formed in my mind, a possible solution.

(*Crowd is heard again off stage* L. RICHARD *enters from cellar
door* L.)

RICHARD.

Sir, if you please . . .

TYSON.

Well, Richard?

(*To him.*)

RICHARD.

I should like to admit
That I've drunk some of the wine put out for the guests.

TYSON.

Well, that's a pretty thing, I must say.

RICHARD.

I was feeling
Low; abominably; about the prisoners
And the row in the street that's getting out of hand.
And certain inner things. And I saw the wine

53

And I thought, well, here goes, and I drank
Three glasses full.

TYSON.

                              I trust you feel better for it?

RICHARD.

I feel much worse. Those two, sir, the prisoners,
What are you doing with them? I don't know why
I keep calling you Sir. I'm not feeling respectful.
If only inflicted pain were as contagious
As a plague, you might use it more sparingly.

(TYSON *backs to* L. *of bench and sits.* CHAPLAIN *rises.*)

TAPPERCOOM.

Who's this cub of a boy?

MARGARET. (*Moves to* RICHARD'S L.)

                              Richard, be sensible.
He's a dear boy but a green boy, and I'm sure
He'll apologise in a minute or two.

TYSON.

                              The boy
Is a silly boy, he's a silly boy; and I'm going
To punish him.

MARGARET.

                    Where are Humphrey and Nicholas?

TYSON.

Now, Margaret . . .

RICHARD.

                    They were where the prisoners are,
Down in the cellars.

MARGARET.

                    Not talking to that witch?

RICHARD.

There isn't a witch. They were sitting about on barrels.
It seemed that neither would speak while the other was there,
And neither would go away. Half an hour ago.
They may be there still.

(*Sits stool* D. L. MARGARET *tries to speak.*)

TYSON. (*Rises.*)

                    I must remind you, Margaret,
That I was speaking to this very stupid boy.
He is going to scrub the floor. Yes, scrub it.

54

Scrub *this* floor *this* evening before our guests
Put in an appearance.
(*Goes to front of desk and writes note.*)
                                    Mulish tasks for a mulish
Fellow. I haven't forgotten his refusal
To fetch the constable.
(CHAPLAIN *sits on bench, facing upstage.*)
RICHARD.

                        Has Alizon Eliot

Been left sitting alone?
MARGARET.

                        Alizon Eliot

Is not for you to be concerned with, Richard.
TYSON.

Am I supposed to be merely exercising my tongue
Or am I being listened to? Do you hear me?
RICHARD. (*Turns to* TYSON.)

Yes; scrub the floor.
(*To* MARGARET.)

                        No, she is not;

I know that.
(*Rises.* MARGARET *sits stool* D. L.)
TYSON. (*Tapping desk.*)

                        Furthermore, you'll relegate
Yourself to the kitchen tonight, fetching and carrying.
If you wish to be a mule you shall be a mule.
(*Comes* D. *to* R. *of* RICHARD *and gives him note.*)
And take this to whatever splendid fellow's
On duty. You will return with the prisoners
And tell them to remain in this room till I send for them.
(*Exit* RICHARD *through cellar door* L.)
Tactics, Tappercoom; the idea that came to me.
You'll think it very good.
✗ TAPPERCOOM.

I am nothing but the justice here, of course,
But perhaps, even allowing for that, you could tell me
What the devil you're up to.
(*Enter* NICHOLAS *through* C. *window, with a gash on his forehead.*
TYSON *moves* R. TAPPERCOOM *rises, facing upstage.*)

NICHOLAS. (*Comes* D. L. *of* CHAPLAIN.)

Look, Chaplain, blood.

Fe fi fo fum. Can you smell it?

MARGARET. (*Moves to them.*)

Now what have you been doing?

NICHOLAS.

Isn't it beautiful?

A splash from the cherry red river that drives my mill!

CHAPLAIN.

Well, yes, it has a cheerful appearance,

(*Rises.*)

But isn't it painful?

MARGARET. (*Puts* NICHOLAS *on* L. *end of bench.*)

I'm sure it's painful.

How did you . . .

(*Enter* HUMPHREY *from stage* L. *through window* C., *stands on* R. *window sill.*)

HUMPHREY.

Mother, I make it known publicly

I'm tired of my little brother. Will you please

Give him to some charity.

NICHOLAS.

Give me faith

And hope and the revolution of our native town.

I've been hit on the head by two-thirds of a brick.

HUMPHREY.

The young fool climbed on the wall and addressed the crowd.

(*Sits on* R. *end of bench.*)

NICHOLAS.

They were getting discouraged. I told them how happy it
    made me

To see them interested in world affairs,

(MARGARET *starts to bandage* NICHOLAS' *head with handkerchief.*)

And how the conquest of evil was being openly

Discussed in this house at that very moment,

And then unfortunately I was hit by a brick.

MARGARET.

What in the world have world affairs

To do with anything? But we won't argue.

56

TYSON. (*Comes above stool.*)

 I believe that brick to have been divinely delivered
 And richly deserved. And am I to understand
 You boys have also attempted conversation
 With the prisoners?

HUMPHREY.

       Now surely, Uncle,
 As one of the Town Council I should be allowed
 To get a grasp of whatever concerns the welfare
 Of the population? Nicholas, I agree,
 Had no business on earth to be down there.

NICHOLAS.

            I was on
 Business of the soul, my sweetheart, business
 Of the soul.

MARGARET.

    You may use that word once too often,
 Nicholas. Heaven or someone will take you seriously
 And then you *would* look foolish. Come with me
 And have your head seen to.

(*Takes* NICHOLAS L. C.)

NICHOLAS. (*Turning to* HUMPHREY.)

        But my big brother
 Was on business of the flesh, by all the fires
 Of Venus, weren't you, Humphrey?

HUMPHREY. (*Rises. They have* CHAPLAIN *between them, but seem about to fight.*)

          What the hell
 Do you mean by that, you little death-watch beetle?

MARGARET.

 Nicholas, will you come?

NICHOLAS.

       Certainly, Mother.

(MARGARET *and* NICHOLAS *go out* U. L.)

TYSON.

 How very remarkably insufferable
 Young fellows can sometimes be. One would expect them
 To care to model themselves on riper minds
 Such as our own, Tappercoom. But really,
 We might as well have not existed, you know.

TAPPERCOOM.

Am I to hear your plan, Tyson, or am I
Just to look quietly forward to old age?

TYSON.

My plan? Ah, yes, my plan! Conclusive and humane.
The two are brought together into this room . . .
How does that strike you?

TAPPERCOOM.

It makes a complete sentence;
Subject: they. Predicate: are brought together . . .

TYSON.

Ah, you will say "with what object?" I'll tell you. We,
That is ourselves, the Chaplain and my elder nephew,
Will remain unobserved in the adjoining room
With the communicating door ajar . . . and how
Does that strike you?

TAPPERCOOM.

With a dull thud, Tyson,
If I may say so.

TYSON.

I see the idea has eluded you.
A hypothetical Devil, Tappercoom,
Brought into conversation with a witch.
A dialogue of hell, perhaps, and conclusive.
Either one or other by their exchange of words
Will prove to be innocent, or we shall have proof
Positive of guilt. Does that seem good?

TAPPERCOOM.

Good is as good results.

HUMPHREY.

I should never have thought
You would have done anything so undignified
As to stoop to keyholes, Uncle.

TYSON.

No, no, no,
The door will be ajar, my boy.

HUMPHREY.

Ah, yes,
That will make us upright.

58

(*Door slams off stage* L. HUMPHREY *rises.*)

> I can hear them coming.

We'd better go.

(*Goes to study door* R., *and opens it.*)

TYSON. (*Rises and moves to study door.*)

> Come along, come along.

(HUMPHREY *exits through study door,* TAPPERCOOM *joins* TYSON *at door. All go round* L. *end of bench.*)

CHAPLAIN. (*Rises.*)

> "The ears of them that hear
> Shall hearken"—The prophet Isaiah.

(TAPPERCOOM *pushes* CHAPLAIN *across.*)

TYSON. (*Upstage of study door.*)

> Come along, Chaplain.

(CHAPLAIN *exits through study door, going between* TYSON *and* TAPPERCOOM. *As soon as he has gone through, he returns during* TAPPERCOOM'S *next speech. They hardly notice him, and he goes* C. *looking for his viol, which he eventually finds at foot of buttress.*)

TAPPERCOOM. (*Downstage of study door, his hand on* TYSON'S *shoulder.*)

> A drink, Tyson. I wish to slake the dryness
> Of my disbelief.

(*Exits study door with* TYSON.)

CHAPLAIN.

> I mustn't leave my mistress.
> Where are you, angel?
> (*Sees viol by buttress and goes to it.*)
> Just where chuckle-head left you.

(*Picks up viol and moves* C. TYSON *has opened study door again, and tries to attract* CHAPLAIN'S *attention, but before he can do so* JENNET *and* THOMAS *enter* D. L. *so he quickly shuts door.* RICHARD *is behind her.*)

RICHARD.

> He wants you to wait here till he sends for you.
> If in some way . . . I wish . . . I must fetch the scrubbers.

(*Exit through door* U. L.)

CHAPLAIN. (*Caught.*)

> Ah . . . ah . . . I'm not really here. I came for

My angel . . . a foolish way to speak of it,
This instrument.
May I say a happy issue
Out of all your afflictions? I hope so. Well,
I'm away now.

(*Goes to door* U. R., *which is locked.*)

THOMAS. (R. *of desk.*)

God bless you, in case you sneeze.

CHAPLAIN. (*Below door* U. R.)
Yes, thank you, I may.

(TYSON *opens study door.*)

And God bless you.

(TYSON *pulls* CHAPLAIN *through study door, then places door ajar.*)

THOMAS. (*To* L. *of window.*)
You would think by the holy scent of it our friend
Had been baptising the garden. But it's only
The heathen rainfall.

(*Sits* L. *window-seat.*)

JENNET.

Do you think he knows
What has been happening to us?

THOMAS.
Old angel scraper?
He knows all right. But he's subdued
To the cloth he works in.

JENNET.
How tired I am. What can you see out there?

THOMAS.
Out here? Out here is a sky so gentle
Five stars have ventured on it. I can see
The sky's pale belly glowing and growing big,
Soon to deliver the moon. And I can see
A glittering smear, the snail-trail of the sun
Where it crawled with its golden shell into the hills.
A darkening land sunken into prayer,
Lucidly, in dew-drops of one syllable,
Nunc dimittis. I see twilight, madam.

JENNET.
What can you hear?

60

THOMAS.

The howl of human jackals.

(*Rises. Enter* RICHARD *from door* U. L., *carrying bucket, floor cloth and knee pad.*)

RICHARD. (L.)

Do you mind? I have to scrub the floor.

THOMAS.

A good old custom.

(*Coming* C.)

Always fornicate

Between clean sheets and spit on a well-scrubbed floor.

(*Sits on bench facing upstage.* RICHARD *crosses to below study door, and kneels, facing upstage.*)

JENNET.

Twilight, double, treble, in and out.

If I try to find my way I bark my brain

On shadows sharp as rocks where half a day

Ago was a wild soft world, a world of warm

Straw whispering every now and then

With rats, but possible, possible, not this

This where I am lost. The morning came and left

The sunlight on my step like any normal

Tradesman. But now every spark

Of likelihood has gone. The light draws off

As easily as though no one could die

Tomorrow.

(RICHARD *starts to wash floor toward buttress.*)

THOMAS.

Are you going to be so serious

About such a mean allowance of breath as life is?

We'll suppose ourselves to be caddis-flies

Who live one day. Do we waste the evening

Commiserating with each other about

The unhygienic condition of our worm-cases?

For God's sake shall we laugh?

JENNET. (*Turns to* THOMAS.)

For what reason?

THOMAS.

For the reason of laughter, since laughter is surely

The surest touch of genius in creation.

61

Would *you* ever have thought of it, I ask you,
If you had been making man, stuffing him full
Of such hopping greeds and passions that he has
To blow himself to pieces as often as he
Conveniently can manage it . . . would it also
Have occurred to you to make him burst himself
With such a phenomenon as cachinnation?
That same laughter, madam, is an irrelevacy
Which almost amounts to a revelation.

JENNET.

                            I laughed
Earlier this evening, and where am I now?

THOMAS.

                                Between
The past and the future which is where you were
Before.

JENNET.

             Was it for laughter's sake you told them
You were the Devil? Or why did you?

(*Sits stool* C.)

THOMAS.

                           Honesty,
Madam, common honesty.

JENNET.

                      Honesty common
With the Devil?

THOMAS.

                Gloriously common. It's Evil, for once
Not travelling incognito. It is what it is.
The Great Unspurious.

JENNET.

                 Thank you for that
You speak of the world I thought I was waking to
This morning. But horror is walking round me here
Because nothing is as it appears to be.
That's the deep water my childhood had to swim in.
My father was drowned in it.

THOMAS.

                    He was drowned in what?
In hypocrisy?

JENNET.

In the pursuit of alchemy.
In refusing to accept the dictum "It is
What it is." Poor father. In the end he walked
In Science like the densest night. And yet
He was greatly gifted.
(RICHARD *on floor washing from buttress along step toward* C.)
When he was born he gave an algebraic
Cry; at one glance measured the cubic content
Of that ivory cone his mother's breast
And multiplied his appetite by five.
So he matured by a progression, gained
Experience by correlation, expanded
Into marriage by contraction, and by
Certain physical dynamics
Formulated me. And on he went
Still deeper into the calculating twilight
Under the twinkling of five-pointed figures
Till Truth became for him the sum of sums
And Death the long division. My poor father.
What years and powers he wasted.
He thought he could change the matter of the world
By strange experiment and by describing
Numerical parabolas.

THOMAS.

To change
The matter of the world! Magnificent!
Intention. And so he died deluded.
(*Sits on floor, leaning against bench.*)

JENNET.

As a matter of fact, it wasn't a delusion.
As a matter of fact, after his death
When I was dusting his laboratory
I knocked over a crucible which knocked
Over another which rocked a third, and they poured
And spattered over some copper coins, which two days later
By impregnation had turned into solid gold.

THOMAS.

Tell that to some sailor on a horse!

63

(RICHARD *takes pail to below window, starts washing from there downstage.*)
   If you had such a secret, I
   And all my fiendish flock, my incubi,
   Succubi, imps and cacodemons, would have leapt
   Out of our bath of brimming brimstone, crying
   ℰureka, *cherchez la femme!* . . . Emperors,
   Would be colonising you, their mistresses
   Patronizing you, ministers of state
   Governmentalising you. And you
   Would be eulogised, lionised, probably
   Canonised for your divine mishap.
JENNET.
   But I never had such a secret. It's a secret
   Still. What it was I spilt, or to what extent,
   Or in what proportion; whether the atmosphere
   Was hot, cold, moist or dry, I've never known.
   And someone else can discolor their fingers, tease
   Their brains and spoil their eyesight to discover it.
   My father broke on the wheel of a dream; he was lost
   In a search. And so for me the actual!
   What I touch, what I see, what I know; the essential fact.
THOMAS.
   In other words, the bare untruth.
JENNET.
                                And, if I may say it
   Without appearing rude, absolutely
   No devils.
THOMAS.
               How in the miserable world, in that case
   Do you come to be here, pursued by the local consignment
   Of fear and guilt? What possible cause . . .
(*Rises, hurting his thumbs as he does so.*)
JENNET.
                                       Your thumbs,
   I'm sure they're giving you pain.
THOMAS. (*Crosses above Jennet, sits in chair* R.)
                           Listen! By both
   My cloven hoofs! If you put us to the rack
   Of an exchange of sympathy, I'll fell you to the ground.

64

Answer my question.

JENNET.

Why do they call me a witch?

Remember my father was an alchemist.
I live alone, preferring loneliness
To the companionable suffocation of an aunt.
I still amuse myself with simple experiments
In my father's laboratory. Also I speak
French to my poodle. Then you must know
I have a peacock which on Sundays
Dines with me indoors. Not long ago
A new little serving-maid carrying the food
Heard its cry, dropped everything and ran,
Never to come back, and told all she met
That the devil was dining with me.

(RICHARD *is now washing steps at* C.)

THOMAS.

It really is
Beyond the limit of respectable superstition
To confuse my voice with a peacock. Don't they know
I sing solo bass in Hell's Madrigal Club?
. . . And as for you, you with no eyes, no ears,
No senses, you the most superstitious
Of all . . . (for what greater superstition
Is there than the mumbo-jumbo of believing
In reality?) . . . you should be swallowed whole by Time
In the way that you swallow appearances.
(*Rises* R. *of* JENNET.)
Horns, what a waste of effort it has been
To give you Creation's vast and exquisite
Dilemma! where altercation thrums
In every granule of the Milky Way,
Persisting still in the dead-sleep of the moon,
And heckling itself hoarse in that hot-head
The sun. And as for here, each acorn drops
Arguing to earth, and pollen's all polemic. . . .
We've given you a world as contradictory
As a female, as cabalistic as the male,
A conscienceless hermaphrodite who plays
Heaven off against hell, hell off against heaven.

65

Revolving in the ball-room of the skies,
Glittering with conflict as with diamonds:
We have wasted paradox and mystery on you
When all you're asking for is cause and effect! . . .
A copy of your birth-certificate was all you needed
To make you at peace with Creation. How uneconomical
The whole thing's been.

(*Goes up to window* L.)

JENNET.

This is a fine time
To scold me for keeping myself to myself and out
Of the clutch of chaos. I was already
In a doorway of perplexity and now
(*Rises.*)
You leave me no escape except
Out on a stream of tears.

(*Sits on floor downstage of bench.*)

THOMAS. (*Moving downstage toward her, falls over* RICHARD'S
legs, and arrives on his knees just L. *of bench.*)
Now, none of that! . . .
(*As he falls.*)

Hell!

RICHARD.
I beg your pardon.

(*Takes bucket slightly upstage and starts washing rostrum step
below desk.*)

THOMAS.

Now that I'm down
On my knees I may as well stay here. In the name
Of all who ever were drowned at sea, don't weep!
I never learnt to swim. May God keep you
From being my Hellespont.

JENNET.

What I do
With my own tears is for me to decide.

THOMAS.
That's all very well. You get rid of them.
But on whose defenceless head are they going to fall?

(*Sits back against stool* L. C.)

66

JENNET.

I had no idea you were so afraid of water.
I'll put them away.

THOMAS.

O Pete, I don't know which
Is worse; to have you crying or to have you behaving
Like Catherine of Aix, who never wept
Until after she was beheaded, and then
The accumulated tears of a long lifetime
Burst from her eyes with such force, they practic'ly winded
Three onlookers and floated the parish priest
Two hundred yards into the entrance hall
Of a brothel.

JENNET. (*Laughs.*)
Poor Catherine.

THOMAS.

Not at all:
It made her life in retrospect infinitely
More tolerable, and when she got to Purgatory
She was laughing so much they had to give her a sedative.

JENNET.

Why should you want to be hanged?

THOMAS.

Madam,
I owe it to myself. But I can leave it
Until the last moment. It will keep
While the light still lasts.

JENNET.

What can we see in this light?
Nothing, I think, except flakes of drifting fear,
The promise of oblivion.

THOMAS.

Nothing can be seen
In the thistledown, but the rough-head thistle comes.
Rest in that riddle. I can pass to you
Generations of roses in this wrinkled berry.
(*Gives her a rose hip, which he takes from his belt.*)
There: now you hold in your hand a race
Of summer gardens, it lies under centuries
Of petals. What is not, you have in your palm.

67

Rest in the riddle, rest; why not? This evening
Is a ridiculous wisp of down
Blowing in the air as disconsolately as dust.
And you have your own damnable mystery, too,
(*Rises.*)
Which at this moment I could well do without.
(*Moves* D. L.)

JENNET.

    I know of none. I'm an unhappy fact
Fearing death. This is a strange moment
To feel my life increasing, when this moment
And a little more may be for both of us
The end of time. You've cast your fishing net
Of eccentricity, your seine of insanity
Caught me when I was already lost
And landed me with despairing gills on your own
Strange beach. That's too inhuman of you.

THOMAS.

                        Inhuman?
If I dared to know what you meant it would be disastrous!

JENNET.

    It means I care whether you live or die,
You have cut yourself a shape in the air, which may be
My scar.

(RICHARD *has moved* C. *below step, washing step.*)

THOMAS.

    Will you stop frightening me to death?
Do you want our spirits to hobble out of their graves
Enduring twinges of hopeless human affection
As long as death shall last? Still to suffer
Pain in the amputated limb? To feel
Passion *in vacuo!* That is the sort of thing
That causes sun-spots, and the Lord knows what
Infirmities in the firmament. I tell you
The heart is worthless,
Nothing more than a pomander's perfume
In the sewerage. And a nosegay of private emotion
Won't distract me from the stench of the plague-pit,
You needn't think it will.

(*Moves across* R., *stepping carefully over* RICHARD'S *legs.*)

68

Excuse me, Richard . . .
Don't entertain the mildest interest in me
Or you'll have me die screaming.
JENNET. (*Sits on bench.*)

Why should that be?
If you're afraid of your shadow falling across
Another life, shine less brightly upon yourself,
Step back into the rank and file of men,
Instead of preserving the magnetism of mystery
And your curious passion for death. You are making your-
self
A breeding ground for love and must take the consequences.
But what are you afraid of, since in a little
While neither of us may exist? Either or both
May be altogether transmuted into memory,
And then the heart's obscure indeed . . . Richard
There's a tear rolling out of your eye. What is it?
RICHARD. (*On floor* c., *looks up at* JENNET.)
Oh, that? I don't really know. I have things on my mind.
JENNET.

Not us?
RICHARD.

Not only.
THOMAS.

If it's a woman, Richard,
Apply yourself to the scrubbing brush. It's all
A trick of the light.
JENNET.

The light of a fire.
(RICHARD *rises*.)
THOMAS.

And, Richard,
Make this woman understand that I
Am a figure of vice and crime . . . .
JENNET.

Guilty of . . .
THOMAS.

Guilty
Of mankind. I have perpetrated human nature.
My father and mother were accessories before the fact,

69

But there'll be no accessories after the fact,
By my virility there won't! Just see me
As I am, me like a perambulating
Vegetable, patched about with inconsequential
Hair, looking out of two small jellies for the means
To live, balanced on folding bones, my sex
No beauty, but a blemish to be hidden
Behind judicious rags, driven and scorched
By boomerang rages and lunacies which never
Touch the accommodating artichoke
Or the seraphic strawberry beaming in its bed;
I defend myself against pain and death by pain
And death, and make the world go round, they tell me,
By one of my less lethal appetites;
Half this grotesque life I spend in a state
Of slow decomposition, using
The name of unconsidered God as a pedestal
On which I stand and bray that I am best
Of beasts, till under some patient
Moon or other I fall to pieces, like
A cake of dung.
            (*Sits stool* C.)
                    Is there a slut would hold
This in her arms and put her lips against it?
JENNET.
    Sluts are only human. By a quirk
Of unastonished nature, your obscene
Decaying figure of vegetable fun
Can drag upon a woman's heart, as though
Heaven were dragging up the roots of hell.
What is to be done? Something compels us into
The terrible fallacy that man is desirable
And there's no escaping into truth. Your crimes
And cruelties leave us longing, and campaigning
Love still pitches his tent of light among
The suns and moons.
    (THOMAS *rises*.)
                    You may be decay and a platitude
Of the flesh, but I have no other such memory of life.
You may be corrupt as ancient apples, well then

70

Corruption is what I most willingly harvest.
You are Evil, Hell, the Father of Lies; if so
Hell is my home, and my days of good were a holiday;
Hell is my hill, and the world slopes away from it
Into insignificance. I have come suddenly
Upon my heart and where it is I see no help for.

THOMAS.

We're lost, both irretrievably lost . . .

(*Enter from study door* TAPPERCOOM, *with the lantern,* TYSON,
HUMPHREY *and* CHAPLAIN. TAPPERCOOM *goes straight to desk, and
puts lantern on upstage end.* RICHARD *goes to* R. *window-seat.*
TYSON *follows* TAPPERCOOM *to desk.* CHAPLAIN *stays below door.*
HUMPHREY *goes* C.)

TAPPERCOOM. (*Entering.*)

                                  Certainly,

The woman has confessed. *Spargere auras
Per vulgam ambigua.* The town can go to bed.

TYSON.

It was a happy idea, eh, Tappercoom? This will be
A great relief to my sister, and everybody
Concerned. A very nice confession, my dear.

THOMAS.

What is this popping noise? Now, what's the matter?

JENNET.

Do they think I've confessed to witchcraft?

HUMPHREY.

                                  Admirably.

CHAPLAIN. (*To* JENNET.)

Bother such sadness, you understand, I'm sure;
Those in authority over us. I should like
To have been a musician but others decreed otherwise
But sin, whatever we might prefer, cannot
Go altogether unregarded.

TAPPERCOOM. (HUMPHREY *has now taken* JENNET *to step* C. *in
front of desk.*)

                                  Now,

Now, Chaplain, don't get out of hand—
Pieties come later.—Young Devize
Had better go and calm the populace.
Tell them faggots will be lit to-morrow at noon.

71

HUMPHREY.

 Have a heart, Mr. Tappercoom; they're hurling bricks.

JENNET. (*Pulls herself free and goes to* THOMAS.)

 What do they mean? Am I at noon to go
 To the fire? Oh, for pity; why must they brand
 Themselves with me!

(*To below buttress.* TYSON *moves to above desk, they all talk.*
THOMAS *goes* U. C. *in front of desk.*)

THOMAS.

 She has bribed you to procure
 Her death! Graft! Graft! Oh, the corruption
 Of this town when only the rich can get to kingdom-
 Come and a poor man is left to groan
 In the full possession of his powers. And she's not
 Even guilty! I demand fair play
 For the criminal classes!

TYSON.

        Terrible state of mind.

 Humphrey, go at once to the gate—

HUMPHREY. (*Goes to* THOMAS, *pulls him toward cellar door* L.)

           Ah, well, I can

 But try to dodge.

THOMAS. (*Knocks* HUMPHREY *down.*)

 You didn't try soon enough!

 (*A crash and door slam off* D. L. CHAPLAIN *moves* L. C.)

 Who else is going to cheat me out of my death?

 (*To* CHAPLAIN.)

 Whee, ecclesiastic, I'll brain you with your wife!

(*Snatches viol from* CHAPLAIN *and chases him downstage below
bench.* TYSON *goes to window* L. JENNET *crosses* D. L. *below
bench.*)

CHAPLAIN. (*Backing from* THOMAS.)

 No, no, with something else, oh please
 Hit me with something else.

(*On knees* L. D. *bench.*)

THOMAS. (*Gives him back viol.*)

            Exchange

 It for a harp and hurry off to heaven. Am I dangerous?
 Will you give me the gallows? . . . Now, *now*, Mr. Mayor!
 Richard, I'll drown him in your bucket.

(Picks up bucket from C. *and takes it to desk.* TYSON *stands on window-seat* L. JENNET *faints on steps* D. L.)

RICHARD. *(Running to* JENNET.)

Look, she's fallen!

CHAPLAIN.

Air! Air!

TYSON.

Water!

THOMAS. *(Crossing* L. C.)

But no fire, do you hear? No fire! . . . How is she, Richard?
Oh, the delicate mistiming of women! She has carefully
Snapped in half my jawbone of an ass.

(TYSON and TAPPERCOOM come D. C. *on step, and* CHAPLAIN *comes to their* R.)

RICHARD.

Life is coming back.

THOMAS.

Importunate life!
It should have something better to do
Than to hang about at a chronic street corner
In dirty weather and worse company.

TAPPERCOOM. *(In* C. *of group.)*

It is my duty as Justice to deliver
Sentence upon you as well.

THOMAS. *(Turning to him.)*

Ah!

TAPPERCOOM.

Found guilty
Of jaundice, misanthropy, suicidal tendencies,
And spearing gloom and despondency. You will spend
The evening joyously, sociably, taking part
In the pleasures of your fellow men.

THOMAS.

Not
Until you've hanged me. I'll be amenable then.

JENNET.

Have I come back to consciousness to hear that
Still?
(Starts to rise.)

Richard, help me to stand . . . You see,

73

Preacher to the caddis-fly, I return
To live my allotted span of insect hours.
But if you batter my wings with talk of death
I'll drop to the ground again.

(THOMAS *helps to seat her on stool* D. L., *then slowly takes his arms away from her, and turns to* TAPPERCOOM. RICHARD *sits on steps* R., D. L.)

THOMAS.

                         Ah, one
Concession to your courage, and then no more.
(*To* TAPPERCOOM L. C.)
Gentlemen, I'll accept your most inhuman
Sentence. I'll not disturb the indolence
Of your gallows yet. But on one condition:
That this lady shall take her share to-night
Of awful festivity. She shall suffer too.

TYSON.

Out of the question. Quite out of the question.
Absolutely out of the question. What, what?

TAPPERCOOM.

What?

THOMAS.

That you shall spend the night in searching
For the bodies of my victims, or else the Lord
Chief Justice of England shall know you let a murderer
Go free. I'll raise the country.

JENNET.

                         Do you think
I can go in gaiety tonight
Under the threat of tomorrow? If I could sleep . . .

THOMAS. (*Crosses to* JENNET.)

That is the heaven to come.
We should be like stars now that it's dark:
Use ourselves up to the last bright dregs
And vanish in the morning. Shall we not
Suffer as wittily as we can? Now, come,
Don't purse your lips up like a little prude at the humor
Of annihilation. It is somewhat broad,
I admit, but we're not children.

74

JENNET.

                                        I am such
A girl of habit. I had got into the way
Of being alive. I will live as well as I can
This evening.

THOMAS.

                    And I'll live, too, if it kills me.
(*Sits* L. *end of bench.*)

HUMPHREY.

Well, Uncle? If you're going to let this clumsy
Fisted cut-throat loose on the house to-night,
Why not the witch-girl, too?
(*Sits on steps* L.)

CHAPLAIN. (*Comes* D. C.)

                                        Foolishly,
I can't help saying it, I should like
To see them dancing.
(TAPPERCOOM *rises, whispers to* TYSON.)

TYSON.

We have reached a decision.
The circumstances compel us reluctantly to
Agree to your most unorthodox request.

THOMAS.

                                        Wisdom

At last. But listen, woman:
(TYSON *whispers to* TAPPERCOOM.)

                                        after this evening
I have no further interest in the world.

JENNET.

My interest also will not be great, I imagine,
After this evening.

QUICK CURTAIN

ACT III

SCENE: *The same, by candlelight and moonlight.*
TIME: *Later, the same night.*
Door U. L. *behind* HUMPHREY *is open, and sounds of the
party can be heard.* THOMAS *appears in passage outside
this door.* HUMPHREY *stands at window-seat* U. C.

THOMAS. (*Entering.*)
O tedium, tedium, tedium.
(*Shuts door.*)

                                  The frenzied
Ceremonial drumming of the humdrum!
Where in this small-talking world can I find
A longitude with no platitude?
(*Sound from* HUMPHREY. THOMAS *sees him and on next
speech moves* U. *to* C. *window and sits on beer barrel* L. *of
it.*)

                                  I must
Apologise. That was no joke to be heard
Making to myself in the full face of the moon.
If only I had been born flame, a flame
Poised say, on the flighty head of a candle,
I could have stood in this draught and gone out,
Whip, through the door of my exasperation.
But I remain, like the possibility
Of water in a desert.

HUMPHREY.
                                  I'm sure nobody
Keeps you here. There's a road outside if you want it.

THOMAS.
What on earth should I do with a road? that furrow
On the forehead of imbecility, a road?
I would as soon be up there, walking in the moon's
White unmolared gums. I'll sit on the world
And rotate with you till we roll into the morning.

HUMPHREY.
You're a pestering parasite. If I had my way

76

You'd be got rid of. You're mad and you're violent,
And I strongly resent finding you slightly pleasant.
(*To stool* D. R.)

THOMAS.

Oh, God, yes, so do I.

(NICHOLAS *enters through door* U. L. *and noise of party can be heard until he closes door. He stands on steps* L.)

NICHOLAS.

As things turn out
I want to commit an offense.

THOMAS.

Does something prevent you?

NICHOLAS.

I don't know what offense to commit.

THOMAS.

What abysmal
Poverty of mind!

NICHOLAS.

This is a night
Of the most asphyxiating enjoyment that ever
Sapped my youth.

HUMPHREY. (*To* NICHOLAS.)

I think I remember
The stars gave you certain rights and interests
In a little blonde religious. How is she, Nicholas?

(*Sits stool* D. R.)

NICHOLAS. (*To* C.)

Your future wife, Humphrey, if that is who
You mean, is pale, tearful and nibbling a walnut.
I loved her once . . . earlier today . . .
Loved her with a passionate misapprehension.
I thought you wanted her, and I'm always deeply
Devoted to your affairs.

(*Sits chair* C.)

But now, I'm bored,

(HUMPHREY *break* R. C.)
As bored as the face of a fish,
In spite of the sunlit barley of her hair.

HUMPHREY.

Aren't I ready to marry her? I thought that was why

We were mooning around here celebrating. What more
Can I do to make you take her off my hands?
And I'm more than ready for the Last Trump as well.
It will stop old Mrs. Cartwright talking.

(*To stool* D. R., *sits.*)

NICHOLAS.

Never.

She's doom itself. She could talk a tombstone off anybody.

(*Enter* MARGARET U. L. *Party sounds can be heard as she closes
door.*)

MARGARET.

Oh, there you are. Whatever's wrong? You both
Go wandering off, as though our guests could be gay
Of their own accord (the few who could bring themselves
To bring themselves, practically in the teeth
Of the recording angel). They're very nervous
And need considerable jollying. Goose liver,
Cold larks, cranberry tart and sucking pig,
And now everyone looks as though they only
Wanted to eat each other, which might in the circumstances
Be the best possible thing. Your uncle sent me
To find you. I can tell he's put out; he's as vexed
As a hen's hind feathers in a wind. And for that
Matter so am I. Go back inside
And be jolly like anyone else's children.

NICHOLAS.

Mother,

I'd as soon kiss the bottom of a Barbary ape.
The faces of our friends may be enchantment
To some, but they wrap my spirits in a shroud.
For the sake of my unborn children I have to avoid them.
Oh, now, be brave, Mother. They'll go in the course of
nature.

MARGARET.

It's unfortunate, considering the wide
Choice of living matter on this globe
That I should have managed to be a mother. I can't
Imagine what I was thinking of. Your uncle
Has made me shake out the lavender
From one of my first gowns which has hung in the wardrobe

78

Four-and-twenty unencouraging years,
To lend to this Jennet girl, who in my opinion
Should not be here. And I said to her flatly
"The course of events is incredible. Make free
With my jewel box." Where is she now?

THOMAS. (*Crosses* D. C., *then* L.)

No doubt

Still making free. Off she has gone
Away to the melting moody horizons of opal,
Moonstone, bloodstone; now moving in lazy
Amber, now sheltering in the shade
Of jade from a brief rainfall of diamonds.
Able to think to-morrow has an even
Brighter air, a glitter less moderate,
A quite unparalleled freedom in the fire:
A death, no bounds to it. Where is she now?
She is dressing, I imagine.

(*Sits stairs* U. L.)

MARGARET.

Yes, I suppose so.

I don't like to think of her.
(*Rises, goes* U. *to* R. *of* THOMAS.)

And as for you

I should like to think of you as someone I knew
Many years ago, and, alas, wouldn't see again.
That would be charming.
(*A step toward* U. L. *door.*)

I beg you to come,

Humphrey. Give your brother a good example.

HUMPHREY.

Mother, I'm unwell.

MARGARET.

Oh, Humphrey!

NICHOLAS.

Mother,

He is officially sick and actually bored.
The two together are as bad as a dropsy.

MARGARET.

I must keep my mind as concentrated as possible
On such pleasant things as the summer I spent at Stoke

D'Abernon. Your uncle must do what he will,
I've done what I can.

(MARGARET *exits* U. L. *and as door opens party sounds can be heard, fading as door is closed.*)

NICHOLAS.

Our Mother isn't
Pleased.

(*Sits chair* L. C.)

HUMPHREY. (*Rises, crosses and sits on chair* C.)
She has never learnt to yawn,
And so she hasn't the smallest comprehension
Of those who can.

THOMAS. (*Rises and moves to stool between chairs and sits.*)
Benighted brothers in boredom
Let us unite ourselves in a toast of ennui,
I give you a yawn: to this evening, especially remembering
Mrs. Cartwright.

(*All yawn.*)
To mortal life, women,
All government, wars, art, science, ambitions
And the entire fallacy of human emotions!

(*As they painfully yawn again, enter* JENNET *bright with jewels and twenty years exquisitely out of fashion. She comes from upstairs,* U. L., *carrying jewel box.*)

JENNET. (*On steps* L.)
And wake us in the morning with an ambrosial
Breakfast, amen, amen.

(*Crosses and sits on stool* D. R.)

NICHOLAS.
Humphrey, poppin,
Draw back the curtains. I have a sense of daylight.

HUMPHREY.
It seems we're facing east.

THOMAS.
You've come too late.
Romulus, Remus and I have just buried the world
Under a heavy snowfall of disinterest.
There's nothing left of life but cranberry tarts,
Goose's liver, sucking pig, cold larks,
And Mrs. Cartwright.

80

JENNET.

That's riches running mad.
What about the have-not moon? Not a goose, not a pig,
And yet she manages to be the wit
Of heaven, and roused the envious Queen of Sheba
To wash in mercury so that the Sheban fountains
Should splash deliriously in the light of her breast.
But she died, poor queen, shining less
Than the milk of her thousand shorthorn cows.

THOMAS. (*Rises and crosses to R. C.*)

What's this?

Where has the girl I spoke to this evening gone
With her Essential Fact? Surely she knows
If she is true to herself, the moon is nothing
But a circumambulating aphrodisiac
Divinely subsidised to provoke the world
Into a rising birth-rate . . . a veneer
Of sheerest Venus on the planks of Time
Which may fool the ocean but which fools not me.

JENNET.

So no moon.

THOMAS.

No moon.

NICHOLAS.

Let her have the last quarter.

JENNET.

No;

If he says no moon then of course there can be no moon.
Otherwise we destroy his system of thought
And confuse the quest for truth.

THOMAS.

You see, Nicholas?

JENNET.

I have only one small silver night to spend,
So show me no luxuries. It will be enough
If you spare me a spider, and when it spins I'll see
The six days of Creation in a web.
And a fly caught on the seventh. And if the dew
Should rise in the web, I may well die a Christian.

81

THOMAS.

I must shorten my sail. We're into a strange wind.
This evening you insisted on what you see,
What you touch, what you know. Where did this weather
   blow from?

JENNET.

Off the moors of mortality; that might
Be so. Or there's that inland sea, the heart . . .
(*On* THOMAS' L.)
But you mustn't hinder me, not now. I come
Of a long-lived family, and I have
Some sixty years to use up almost immediately.
I shall join the sucking pig.

(D. C. *on stage level.*)

NICHOLAS.

                              Please take my arm.
I'll guide you there.

HUMPHREY.

                         He shall do no such thing.
Who's the host here?

THOMAS. (*Moves* D. R.)

                         They have impeccable manners
When they reach a certain temperature.

HUMPHREY.

                                        A word
More from you, and you go out of this house.

THOMAS.

Like the heart going out of me, by which it avoids
Having to break.

(*Sits on stool* D. R. *Viol heard off stage* U. L., *playing a slightly
religious dance.* HUMPHREY *and* NICHOLAS *move toward door.*
HUMPHREY *to* L. *of door.*)

JENNET.

                      Be quiet for a moment. I hear
A gay modulating anguish, rather like music.

NICHOLAS.

It's the Chaplain, extorting lightness of heart
From the guts of his viol, to the greater glory of God.

(TYSON *enters from door* U. L., *leaving it open. Party noise is
heard mixed with the music. He enters between* NICHOLAS *and*

HUMPHREY, *speaking as he comes, and goes* L. C.)

TYSON.

What I hear from your mother isn't agreeable to me
In the smallest.

(*Sees* JENNET.)

A draught, quite noticeable.
I'm a victim to air.

(*Sits chair* L. C. TYSON *motions* NICHOLAS *to close* U. L. *door,
which he does, the party sounds stop, but viol continues
slightly softer, and more in dance tempo.*)

I expect members of my family . . .

THOMAS.

Is this courtesy, Mr. Mayor, to turn your back
On a guest?

JENNET. (R. *of* C. *chair.*)

Why should I be welcome? I am wearing
His days gone by. I rustle with his memories!
I, the little heretic, as he thinks,
The all unhallows Eve to his poor Adam;
And nearly stubbing my toes against my grave
In his sister's shoes, the grave he has ordered for me.
Don't ask impossibilities of the gentleman.

TYSON.

Humphrey, will you explain yourself?

HUMPHREY.

Uncle,
I came to cool my brow. I was on my way back.

NICHOLAS.

Don't keep us talking. I need to plunge again
Into that ice-cap of pleasure in the next room.

(*Holds out arm to* JENNET.)

I repeat, my arm.

HUMPHREY. (D. L. *on step.*)

I repeat that I am the host.

I have the right . . .

JENNET. (*On steps.*)

He has the right, Nicholas.

(*Crosses to between them.*)

Let me commit no solecism so near
To eternity. Please open the door for us.

83

(NICHOLAS *opens* U. L. *door, goes through and holds it open. The party can be heard, growing into exclamations as* JENNET *appears to them.* JENNET *holds out her hand to* HUMPHREY *and they exit together* U. L. NICHOLAS *shuts door, and sounds cease.*)

We must go in as smoothly as old friends.

THOMAS.

Well, does your blood run deep enough to run
Cold, or have you none?

(*Cross to* R. *of* TYSON.)

TYSON. (*Facing away from* THOMAS.)

                        That's enough. Go away.

THOMAS.

    Are you going to cry-off the burning?

TYSON.

                            Worthless creatures,
Both; I call you clutter. The standard soul
Must mercilessly be maintained. No
Two ways of life. One God, one point of view,
A general acquiescence to the mean.

THOMAS.

And God knows when you say the mean, you mean
The mean. You'd be surprised to see the number
Of cloven hoofmarks in the yellow snow of your soul.
And so you'll kill her.
Time would have done it for her, too, of course,
But more cautiously and with a pretence of charm.
Am I allowed in bail into your garden?

(*Turns upstage.*)

TYSON. (*Blows his nose.*)

    Tiresome catarrh; go where you like.

THOMAS.

    That's nowhere in this world.
But I still maybe
Can make myself useful and catch mice for an owl.

(*Moves* U. *to window.* TAPPERCOOM *enters* U. L. *and comes* L. THOMAS *exits through window,* C., *going off* L.)

TAPPERCOOM.

    The young lunatic slipping off, is he?
Cheered up and gone? So much the less trouble for us.

84

(Puts empty tankard he is carrying on table.)
Very jolly evening, Tyson.
(Taps Tyson on back and crosses to C.)
Are you sober?

TYSON. *(Crying.)*
Yes, yes, yes.

TAPPERCOOM. *(Sits* C.)
You shouldn't say that, you know.
You're in tears, Tyson. I know when I see them,
My wife has them. You've drunk too deep, my boy.
Now I'm as sober as a judge, perhaps a judge
A little on circuit, but still sober. Tyson,
You're in tears, old fellow, two little wandering
Jews of tears getting 'emselves embrangled
In your beard.

TYSON.
I won't stand it, Tappercoom:
I won't have it, I won't have evil things
Looking so distinguished. I'm no longer
Young, and I should be given protection.

TAPPERCOOM.
What
Do you want protecting from now?

TYSON.
We must burn her,
Before she destroys our reason. Damnable glitter.
Tappercoom, we mustn't become bewildered
At our time of life. Too unusual
Not to be corrupt.
(Rises and crosses to fire.)
Must be burnt
Immediately, burnt, burnt, Tappercoom,
Immediately.
(Sits stool D. R.)

TAPPERCOOM.
Are you trying to get rid of temptation,
Tyson? A belated visit of the wanton flesh
After all these years? You've got to be dispassionate.
Calm and civilized. I am civilized.
I know, frinstance, that Beauty is not an Absolute.

85

Beauty is a Condition. As you might say
Hey nonny yes or Hey nonny no.
But the Law's as aboute an Absolute . . .

(CHAPLAIN *enters from door* U. L., *carrying viol. Party can be heard, stops immediately door is closed after him.* TAPPER-COOM *sees* CHAPLAIN L.)

Hello, feeling dickey, Chaplain?

CHAPLAIN. (*Coming* D. *to chair* C. L.)

It would be
So kind if you didn't notice me. I have
Upset myself. I have no right to exist,
Not in any form, I think.

(*Sits chair* C. L.)

TAPPERCOOM.

I hope you won't
Think me unsociable if I don't cry myself.
What's the matter? Here's the pair of you
Dripping like newly weighed anchors.
Let the butterflies come to you, Chaplain.
Or you'll never be pollinated into a Bishop.

CHAPLAIN.

No, it's right and it's just that I should be cast down.
I've treated her with an abomination
That maketh desolate: . . . the words, the words
Are from Daniel . . .

TAPPERCOOM.

Hey, what's this? The young woman again?

CHAPLAIN.

My patient instrument. I made my viol
Commit such sins of sound . . . and I didn't mind:
No, I laughed. I was trying to play a dance.
I'm too unaccomplished to play with any jollity.
I shouldn't venture beyond religious pieces.

(*Kisses his viol.*)

TYSON.

There's no question of jollity. We've got
To burn her, for our peace of mind.

TAPPERCOOM.

You must wait
Until tomorrow, like a reasonable chap.

86

And to-morrow, remember, you'll have her property
Instead of your present longing for impropriety.
And her house, now I come to think of it
Will suit me nicely.

(*Rises.*)

A large mug of small beer for both of you.
Leave it to me.

(*Crosses behind chairs to* L.)

CHAPLAIN. (*Getting up.*)

No, no, no,
I should become delighted again. I wish
For repentance . . .

(RICHARD *enters* U. L. *He stands* R. *of door* U. L. CHAPLAIN *moves to steps* L.)

TAPPERCOOM.

You shall have it. I'll pour it out.
Myself. You'll see; it shall bring you to your knees.

CHAPLAIN. (*On steps* L.)

I'm too unaccomplished. I haven't the talent.
But I hoped I should see them dancing. And after all
They didn't dance . . .

TAPPERCOOM.

They shall, dear saint, they shall.

(*They exit* U. L. RICHARD *opens door for them, then shuts it and crosses to* TYSON.)

RICHARD.

I was sent to tell you, Mr. Tyson . . .

TYSON.

I'm not
To be found. I'm fully occupied elsewhere.

(*Rises and crosses to study door.*)

If you wish to find me I shall be in my study.

(RICHARD *opens study door* R. *for* TYSON.)

You can knock, but I shall give you no reply.
I wish to be alone with my convictions.
Good night.

(*He exits.* RICHARD *shuts study door, moves to table.* THOMAS *looks through window, and stands on window sill.*)

THOMAS.

The Great Bear is looking so geometrical

One would think that something or other could be proved.
Are you sad, Richard?

RICHARD.

Certainly.

(*Sits on stool below table.*)

THOMAS.

I also.
I've been cast adrift on a raft of melancholy.
The night wind passed me, like a sail across
A blind man's eye. There it is,
The interminable tumbling of the great grey
Main of moonlight, washing over
The little oyster-shell of this month of April:
Among the raven-quills of the shadows
And on the white pillows of men asleep:
The night's a pale pasture land of peace,
And something condones the world incorrigibly.

(*Sits on window-seat* R.)

But what, in fact, is this vaporous charm?
We're softened by a nice conglomeration
Of the world's uneven surface, refraction of light,
Obstruction of light, condensation, distance,
And that sappy upshot of self-centered vegetablism,
The trees of the garden. How is it we come
To see this as a heaven in the eye?
Why should we hawk, and spit out ecstasy
As though we were nightingales, and call these quite
Casual degrees and differences
Beauty? What guile recommends the world
And gives our eyes a special sense to be
Deluded above all animals? . . . Stone me, Richard!
I've begun to talk like that soulless girl, and she
May at this moment be talking like me! I shall go
Back into the garden, and choke myself with the seven
Sobs I managed to bring with me from the wreck.

RICHARD.

To hear her you would think her feet had almost
Left the ground.

(*Rises and moves to behind chair* C.)

The evening which began

88

So blackly, now, as though it were a kettle
Set over her flame, has started to sing. And all
The time I find myself praying under my breath
That something will save her.

THOMAS. (*Moving up* C.)
You might do worse,
Tides turn with a similar sort of whisper.

(*Stands at* R. *window-sill. Door* U. L. *opens and we hear the party again.* ALIZON *enters quickly, shuts door and the sounds cease.*)

ALIZON. (*Just inside door.*)
Richard!

RICHARD.
Alizon!

ALIZON.
I've come to be with you.

RICHARD.
Not with me. I'm the to-and-fro-fellow
Tonight. You have to be with Humphrey.

ALIZON.
I think
I have never met Humphrey. I have met him less
And less the more I have seen him.

THOMAS.
You will forgive me.
I was mousing for a small Dutch owl.
If it has said towoot t-wice it has said it
A thousand times.

(*Exit quickly through window, and off* L.)

RICHARD. (*Up to window, looks after* THOMAS.)
Hey! Thomas!
. . . Ah, well.

(*Comes slowly down* C.)
The crickets are singing well with their legs tonight.

ALIZON. (*Below chair* L.)
It sounds as though the night air were riding
On a creaking saddle.

RICHARD.
You must go back to the others.

89

ALIZON.

    Let me stay. I'm not able to love them.

    Have you forgotten what they mean to do tomorrow?

RICHARD.

                  How could I forget? But there are laws

    And if someone fails them . . .

ALIZON.

                                I shall run

    Away from laws if laws can't live in the heart.

    I shall be gone tomorrow.

RICHARD. (*To her.*)

                        You make the room

    Suddenly cold. Where will you go?

ALIZON.

                       Where

    Will you come to find me?

RICHARD.

                     Look, you've pulled the thread

    In your sleeve. Is it honest for me to believe

    You would be unhappy?

ALIZON.

                When?

RICHARD.

                   If you marry Humphrey?

ALIZON.

    Humphrey's a winter in my head.

    But whenever my thoughts are cold and I lay them

    Against Richard's name, they seem to rest

    On the warm ground where summer sits

    As golden as a humblebee.

    So I did very little but think of you

    Until I ran out of the room.

RICHARD.

                  Do you come to me

    Only because you can never love the others?

ALIZON.

                      Our father

    God moved many lives to show you to me.

    I think that is the way it must have happened.

    It was complicated, but very kind.

RICHARD. (*Makes slight turn away, then back again.*)

                                     If I asked you
    If you could ever love me, I should know
    For certain that I was no longer rational.

ALIZON.

    I love you quite as much as I love St. Anthony,
    And rather more than I love St. John Chrysostom.

RICHARD.

    But putting haloes on one side, as a man
    Could you love me, Alizon?

(*Kneels on her* R.)

ALIZON.

                             I have become
    A woman, Richard, because I love you. I know
    I was a child three hours ago. And yet
    I love you as deeply as many years could make me,
    But less deeply than many years will make me.

RICHARD. (*Kisses her.*)

    I think I may never speak steadily again,
    What have I done or said to make it possible
    That you should love me?

ALIZON.

                       Everything I loved
    Before has come to one meeting place in you,
    And you have gone out into everything I love.

RICHARD.

    Happiness seems to be weeping in me, as
    I suppose it should, being newly born.

ALIZON.

    We must never leave each other now, or else
    We should perplex the kindness of God.

RICHARD.

                          The kindness

    Of God itself is not a little perplexing.
    What do we do?

ALIZON.

                  We cleave to each other, Richard.
    That is what is proper for us to do.

RICHARD.

    But you were promised to Humphrey, Alizon.

(*Crosses to her* L.)
And I'm hardly more than a servant here,
Tied to my own apron strings. They'll never
Let us love each other.
(*Turns back to her.*)
ALIZON.

                     Then they will have
To outwit all that ever went to create us.
RICHARD. (*Taking her hands in his.*)
So they will. I believe it. Let them storm.
We're lovers in a deep and safe place
And never lonely any more. . . . Alizon,
Shall we make the future, however much it roars,
Lie down with our happiness? Are you ready
To forego custom and escape with me?
ALIZON.

Shall we go now, before anyone prevents us?
RICHARD. (*Moves to* U. L. *door and back to* ALIZON.)
I'll take you to the old priest who first found me.
He is as near to being my father
As putting his hand into a poor-box could make him.
He'll help us. Oh, Alizon, I so
Love you.
     (*Kisses her, takes her* R. *to below door* U. R.)
               Let yourself quietly out and wait for me
Somewhere near the gate, but move in a shadow.
I must fetch my savings. Are you afraid?
ALIZON.

                     In some
Part of me, not all; and while I wait
I can have a word with the saints Theresa and Christopher:
They may have some suggestions.
RICHARD.

                   Yes, do that.
Now: like a mouse.
(*Gives her a quick kiss.* ALIZON *exits* U. R. *and off.* RICHARD
goes to the window.)
              Only let me spell
No disillusion for her, safety, peace,
And a good world, as good as she has made it!

92

(*Moves* C. MARGARET *enters from* U. L., *and party is heard again,
stopping as door is closed. She crosses to* RICHARD, *who stops as
he sees her.*)

MARGARET.

Now, Richard, have you found Mr. Tyson?

RICHARD.

Yes,

He's busy with his convictions.

(*Crosses* MARGARET.)

MARGARET.

He has no business

To be busy now. How am I to prevent

This girl, condemned as a heretic, from charming us

With gentleness, consideration and gaiety?

It makes orthodoxy seem almost irrelevant.

But I expect they would tell us the soul can be as lost

For loving-kindness as in anything else.

Well, well; we must scramble for grace as best we can.

Where is Alizon?

RICHARD.

I must . . . I must . . .

MARGARET.

The poor child has gone away to cry,

See if you can find her, will you, Richard?

RICHARD.

I have to . . . have to . . .

(*Makes a quick exit out cellar door* L.)

MARGARET.

Very well, I will go

In search of the sad little soul, myself.

(*Looks around, looks upstairs,* U. L., *and sighs.*)

Oh dear, I could do with a splendid holiday

In a complete vacuum.

(*Exit upstairs* U. L. JENNET *enters from door* U. L. *She seems for
a moment exhausted, but crosses to the windows. She is followed
by* NICHOLAS *and* HUMPHREY. *Party can be heard again, stopping
as door is closed.*)

NICHOLAS.

Are you tired of us?

93

HUMPHREY.

                               Why on earth
    Can't you stop following her?

NICHOLAS.

                             Stop following me.

JENNET. (*Looking out of window.*)
    I am troubled to find Thomas Mendip.

(NICHOLAS *is on* JENNET'S L. *by window,* HUMPHREY *on*
NICHOLAS' L.)

NICHOLAS.

                         He's far gone . . .
    As mad as the nature of man.

HUMPHREY.

                       As rude and crude
    As an act of God. He'll burn your house.

JENNET.

                     So he has. . . .

    (*Comes down to fire.*)
    Are you kind to mention burning?

HUMPHREY.

                     I beg your pardon.

NICHOLAS. (*To* JENNET'S L.)
    Couldn't you tomorrow by some elementary spell
    Reverse the direction of the flames and make them burn
        downwards?
    It would save you unpleasantness and increase at the same
    Time the heat below, which would please
    Equally heaven and hell.

    (HUMPHREY *comes downstage with* NICHOLAS, *but further* C.)
    I feel such a tenderness for you, not only because
    I think you've bewitched my brother, which would be
    A most salutary thing, but because, even more
    Than other women, you carry a sense of that cavernous
    Night folded in night, where Creation sleeps
    And dreams of men. If only we loved each other
    Down the pitshaft of love I could go
    To the motive mysteries under the soul's floor
    Well drenched in damnation I should be as pure
    As a limewashed wall.

(JENNET *sits stool.* NICHOLAS *kneels.*)

HUMPHREY. (*A step toward them.*)

Get out!

(*Pushes* NICHOLAS R. C.)

JENNET.

He does no harm . . .
Is it possible he still might make for death
Even on this open-hearted night?

HUMPHREY. (*Crossing to buttress.*)

Who might?

JENNET.

Thomas Mendip. He's sick of the world, but the world
Has a right to him.

HUMPHREY.

Damn Thomas Mendip.

NICHOLAS.

Nothing

Easier.

(HUMPHREY *cross to below buttress. Enter* RICHARD *from
cellar door* L., *carrying his possessions tied in a handkerchief.
He is upset to see his escape is cut off.*)

You're just the fellow, Richard.

(*Crosses to him.*)

We need some more Canary, say five bottles
More. And before we go in, we'll drink here, privately,
To beauty and the sombre sultry waters
Where beauty haunts.

RICHARD. (*Tries to cross* NICHOLAS.)

I have to find . . . to find . . .

NICHOLAS. (*Stopping him and pushing him* D. L.)

Five bottles of Canary. I'll come to the cellars
And help you bring them. Quick, before our Mother
Calls us back to evaporate into duty.

(NICHOLAS *pushes* RICHARD *off* L., *and exits.*)

HUMPHREY. (*Moves* D. *to* R. *of* JENNET.)

He's right. You have bewitched me. But not by scents
Of new-mown hell. For all I know you may
Have had some by-play with the Devil, and your eyes
May well be violets in a stealthy wood
Where souls are lost. If so, you will agree

95

The fire is fair, as far goes: you have
To burn.

JENNET.

It is hard to live last hours.
As the earth deserves. Must you bring closer the time
When, as night yawns under my feet,
I shall be cast away in the chasm of dawn?
I am tired with keeping my thoughts clear of that verge.

HUMPHREY.

But need you? These few hours of the night
Might be lived in a way which wouldn't end
In fire. It would be insufferable
If you were burned while you were strange to me.
I should never sit at ease in my body again.

JENNET.

Must we talk of this? All there is
To be said has been said, and all in a heavy sentence;
There's nothing to add except a grave silence.

HUMPHREY. (*Rises, moving* D. C.)

Listen, will you listen? There is more to say,
(*Breaks* L., *then leans on back of chair* L., *facing her.*)
I am able to save you,
(JENNET *sits chair* C.)
                                   since all official action
Can be given official hesitation. I happen
To be on the Council, and a dozen reasons
Can be found to postpone the moment of execution:
Legal reasons, monetary reasons . . .
They've confiscated your property, and I can question
Whether your affairs may not be too disordered.
And once postponed, a great congestion of quibbles
Can be let loose over the Council table . . .

JENNET.

Hope can break the heart, Humphrey. Hope
Can be too strong.

HUMPHREY.

                  But this is true: actual
As my body is. And as for that . . . now, impartially
Look what I risk.
(*Sits in chair* L. C.)

96

If in any way you've loosened
The straps which hold in place our fairly workable
Wings of righteousness, and they say you have,
When my status in both this town and the after-life
Will be gone if either suspect me of having helped you
I have to be given a considerable reason
For risking that.

JENNET.

I fondly hope I'm beginning
To misconstrue you.

HUMPHREY. (*Rises and crosses in front of her to kneel on her* R.)
Later on tonight
When they've all gone small into their beauty sleep
I'll procure the key and come to your cell. Is that
Agreeable?

JENNET.

Is it so to you?
Aren't you building your castles in foul air?

HUMPHREY.
Foul? No; it's give and take, the basis
Of all understanding.

JENNET.

You mean you give me a choice:
To sleep with you, or tomorrow to sleep with my fathers.
(HUMPHREY *shrugs.*)
And if I value the gift of life,
Which, dear heaven, I do, I can scarcely refuse.

HUMPHREY. (*Laughs.*)
Isn't that sense?

JENNET.

Admirable sense.
Oh, why, why am I not sensible?
Oddly enough, I hesitate. Can I
So dislike being cornered by a young lecher
That I would rather die? That would be
The maniac pitch of pride. Indeed it might
Even be sin. Can I believe my ears?
I seem to be considering heaven. And heaven,
From this angle, seems considerable.

HUMPHREY. (*Rises and leans over* JENNET's *chair.*)

97

Now, please, we're not going to confuse the soul and the body.
This, speaking bodily, is merely an exchange
Of compliments.

JENNET.

And surely throwing away
My life for the sake of pride would seem to heaven
A bodily blasphemy, a suicide?

HUMPHREY.

Even if heaven were interested. Or even
If you cared for heaven.

(HUMPHREY *tries to kiss* JENNET, *she rises and moves to below chair* L.)

Am I unattractive to you?

JENNET.

Except that you have the manners of a sparrowhawk,
With less reason, no, you are not.

(HUMPHREY *takes a step toward her, she crosses to* R. C.)

But even so
I'd no more run to your arms than I wish to run
To death. I ask myself why. Surely I'm not
Mesmerised by some snake of chastity?

HUMPHREY.

This isn't the time . . .

JENNET.

Don't speak, contemptible boy,
I'll tell you: I am not. We have
To look elsewhere . . . for instance, into my heart
Where recently I heard begin a
Bell of longing which calls no one to church.
But need that, ringing away in vain,
Drown the milkmaid singing in my blood
And freeze into the tolling of my knell?
That would be pretty, indeed, but unproductive.
No, it's not that.

HUMPHREY. (*To above chair* C.)

Jennet, before they come
And interrupt us . . .

JENNET. (*Crosses to above fire.*)

I am interested
In my feelings, I seem to wish to have some importance

98

In the play of time. If not,
Then sad was my mother's pain, sad my breath,
Sad the articulation of my bones,
Sad, sad my alacritous web of nerves,
Woefully, woefully sad my wondering brain,
To be shaped and sharpened into such tendrils
Of anticipation, to feed the swamp of space.
What is deep as love is deep, I'll have
Deeply. What is good as love is good
I'll have well. Then if time and space
Have any purpose, I shall belong to it.
If not, if all is a pretty fiction
To distract the cherubim and seraphim
Who so continually do cry, the least
I can do is to fill the curled shell of the world
With human deep-sea sound, and hold it to
The ear of God, until he has appetite
To taste our salt sorrow on his lips.
(*Sits stool.*)
And so you see it might be better to die.
(HUMPHREY *goes to her, kneels* R. *of her.*)
Though on the other hand, I admit it might
Be immensely foolish.
    (*A thundering noise from understage* D. L.)
               Listen! What
    Can all the thundering from the cellars be?
(HUMPHREY *moves* C. JENNET *goes quickly to study door, then
back to buttress, when caught by* HUMPHREY.)
HUMPHREY.
    I don't know at all.
    (*Goes to her.*)
               You're simply playing for time.
    (*Seizes her.*)
    Why can't you answer me before I'm thrown
By the bucking of my pulse, before Nicholas
Interrupts us? Will it be all right?
JENNET.
    Doesn't my plight seem pitiable to you?
HUMPHREY. (*Leaning over her.*)
    Pitiable, yes. It makes me long for you

Intolerably. Now, be a saint, and tell me
I may come to your cell.
(THOMAS *appears in window, climbs in and stands on window-
seat* R.)

I wish I could believe
My freedom was not in the flames. Oh God, I wish
The ground would open.

THOMAS. (*Coming down* R. *and pulling* HUMPHREY *away, throws
him on step* L. *of buttress.*)

Allow me to open it for you!
Admit I was right. Man's a mistake.
Lug-worms the lot of us.
(*Stands with one foot on* HUMPHREY's *chest.*)
HUMPHREY.

Wipe your filthy boots
Before you start trespassing.

THOMAS. (*Takes off his coat and throws it on* R. *window-seat.*)

And as for you,
I'll knock your apple-blossom back into the roots
Of the Tree of Knowledge where you got it from!
(*Crosses to* R. *below step.* HUMPHREY *rises.*)
JENNET.

Oh dear,
Is it lug-worms at war?
(*To* THOMAS.)

And by what right, will you tell me,
Do your long ears come moralizing in
Like Perseus to Andromeda? Pause a moment
And consider.
THOMAS.

Madam, if I were Herod in the middle
Of the massacre of the innocents, I'd pause
Just to consider the confusion of your imagery.
HUMPHREY.

If he wants to fight me, let him. Come out into the garden.
Whatever happens I shall have one bash at him
(THOMAS *moves to below passageway leading to door* U. R.)
Which, next to this other thing, is the most desirable
Act in the world. If he kills me, you and I
The day after tomorrow, can improve

100

The deadly hours of the grave
By thrashing out the rights and wrongs of it.
(THOMAS *moves to* C. *stage,* HUMPHREY *to study door.*)
Only remember, I thought you unfairly beautiful
And, to balance your sins, you should be encouraged
For heaven's sake to spend your beauty
In a proper way, on someone who knows its worth.

THOMAS.
Sound the trumpets!

JENNET.
                    Yes, why not! And a roll
Of drums. You, if you remember, failed
Even to give me a choice. You have only said
"Die, woman, and look as though you liked it."
So you'll agree this can hardly be said to concern you.

(*Crossing downstage* L. C.)

THOMAS. (U. R. *of chair* C.)
All right! You've done your worst. You force me to tell you
The disastrous truth. I love you. A misadventure
So intolerable, hell could do no more.
Nothing in the world could touch me
And you have to come and be the damnable
Exception. I was nicely tucked up for the night
Of eternity, and like a restless dream
Of a fool's paradise, you, with a rainbow where
Your face is, and an *ignis fatuus*
Worn like a rose in your girdle, come pursued
By fire, and presto! the bedclothes are on the floor
And I, the tomfool, love you. Don't say again
That this doesn't concern me, or I shall say
That you needn't concern yourself with tomorrow's burning.

(*Enter* NICHOLAS *from cellar door* L., *carrying five bottles of Canary wine.*)

NICHOLAS.
Do you know what that little bastard Richard did?
He locked me in the cellars.

(*Standing near* L. *door.*)

THOMAS.
                    Don't complicate
The situation . . . I love you, perfectly knowing

101

You're nothing but a word out of the mouth
Of that same planet of almighty blemish
Which I long to leave. But the word is an arrow
Of larksong, shot from the earth's bow, and falling
In a stillborn sunrise . . . I shall lie in my grave
With my hands clapped over my ears, to stop your music
From riddling me as much as the meddling worms.
(HUMPHREY *rises*. JENNET *sits chair* L.)
Still, that's beside the point. We have to settle
This other matter.

NICHOLAS. (*Going upstage of chairs between them.*)
                                    Yes, I was telling you.
I went into the cellars to get the wine,
And the door swung after me, and that little son
Of a crossbow turned the key . . .
(*Puts bottles under table.*)
THOMAS. (*Sits on chair* C., *to* JENNET.)
                                    Can we find somewhere
To talk where there isn't quite so much insect life?
(HUMPHREY *sits by buttress again*.)
NICHOLAS.
      And there I was, in cobwebs up to my armpits,
      Hammering the door and yelling like a slaughter-house
      Until the cook came and let me out. Where is he?
JENNET.
      What should we talk of? You mean to be hanged.
      Am I to understand that your tongue-tied dust
      Will slip a ring on the finger of my ashes
      And we'll both die happily ever after? Surely
      His other suggestion, though more conventional,
      Has fewer flaws?
THOMAS.
                        But you said, like a ray of truth
      Itself, that you'd rather burn.
JENNET.
                                    My heart, my mind
      Would rather burn. But may not the casting vote
      Be with my body? And is the body necessarily
      Always ill-advised?

102

NICHOLAS. (*Rises and stands slightly upstage of them, but be-tween them.*)

> Something has happened
> Since I made the descent into those hellish cobwebs.
> I'm adrift. What is it?

THOMAS.

> Let me speak to her.

(NICHOLAS *crosses to* L. *of* HUMPHREY.)

> You've destroyed my defences, the laborious contrivance
> Of hours, the precious pair of you. Oh Jennet,
> (*Rises.*)
> Jennet, you should have let me go before
> I confessed a word of this damned word love. I'll not
> Reconcile myself to a dark world
> (JENNET *rises.*)
> For the sake of five-foot six of wavering light,
> For the sake of a woman who goes no higher
> Than my bottom lip.

NICHOLAS.

> I'll strip and fly my shirt
> At the masthead unless someone picks me up.
> What has been going on?

THOMAS. (C. *on step. Points to* HUMPHREY.)

> Ask that neighing
> Horse-box-kicker there, your matchless brother.

NICHOLAS. (*Puts his arm around* HUMPHREY.)

> Ah, Humphrey, darling, have there been
> Some official natural instincts?

HUMPHREY. (*Crosses down and sits on stool* D. R.)

> I've had enough.
> The whole thing's become unrecognisable.

JENNET. (*Moves up to* L. *of* THOMAS.)

> Have I a too uncertain virtue to keep you
> On the earth?

THOMAS.

> I ask nothing, nothing. Stop
> Barracking my heart. Save yourself
> His way if you must. There will always be
> Your moment of hesitation, which I shall chalk
> All over the walls of purgatory. Never mind

That, loving you, I've trodden the garden threadbare
Completing a way to save you.

(*Crosses* D. L. *and sits on step.*)

JENNET.

                       If you saved me
Without wishing to save yourself, you might have saved
Your trouble.

(*Sits on chair* L.)

NICHOLAS. (*Upstage of* HUMPHREY.)

I imagine it's all over with us, Humphrey.
I shall go and lie with my own thoughts
And conceive reciprocity. Come on, you boy of gloom,
The high seas for us.

HUMPHREY.

                 O, go and drown yourself
And me with you.

NICHOLAS.

              There's no need to drown,
We'll take the tails off mermaids.

(*To buttress. Enter* MARGARET *from upstairs,* D. L., *stands at foot of steps.*)

MARGARET.

         Have any of you seen
That poor child Alizon? I think
She must be lost.

NICHOLAS. (*Sitting on buttress.*)

              Who isn't? The best
Thing we can do is to make wherever we are lost in
Look as much like home as we can. Now don't
Be worried. She can't be more lost than she was with us.

HUMPHREY.

I can't marry her, mother. Could you think
Of something else to do with her?
I'm going to bed.

NICHOLAS.

        I think Humphrey has been
Improperly making a proper suggestion, mother.
He wishes to be drowned.

MARGARET. (*To* THOMAS.)

            They find it impossible

104

To concentrate. Have you seen the little
Fairhaired girl?

NICHOLAS.

He wishes to be hanged.

MARGARET. (*Crosses to* JENNET.)

Have you hidden the child?

(*Crosses R. C. as* NICHOLAS *speaks.*)

NICHOLAS.

She wishes to be burned
Rather than sleep with my brother.

MARGARET.

She should be thankful
She can sleep at all. For years I have woken up
Every quarter of an hour. I must sit down.
(*Sits on C. chair.*)
I'm too tired to know what anyone's saying.

JENNET.

I think none of us knows where to look for Alizon.
Or for anything else.
(*Rises, crosses to* MARGARET.)

But shall we, while we wait
For news of her, as two dispirited women
Ask this man to admit he did no murders?

(JENNET *and* MARGARET *look at* THOMAS, *who moves toward window C.*)

THOMAS.

You think not?

JENNET.

I know. There was a soldier,
Discharged and centerless, with a towering pride
In his sensibility, and an endearing
Disposition to be a hero, who wanted
To make an example of himself to all
Erring mankind, and falling in with a witch-hunt
His good heart took the opportunity
Of providing a diversion.
(JENNET *moves C.*)

O Thomas,
It was very theatrical of you to choose the gallows.

105

THOMAS. (*To* MARGARET.)

    Mother, we won't listen to this girl.

    She is jealous, because of my intimate relations

    With damnation. But damnation knows

    I love her.

(RICHARD *enters* U. R.)

RICHARD.

               We have come back.

NICHOLAS. (*Crossing toward* RICHARD.)

    I want to talk to you. Who locked me in the cellars?

(ALIZON *enters,* U. R., *behind* RICHARD.)

MARGARET.

    Alizon, where have you been?

ALIZON.

               We had to come back.

MARGARET.

    Back? From where?

RICHARD. (*Stepping forward.*)

               We came across Old Skipps.

ALIZON. (*To* MARGARET.)

    We were running away. We wanted to be happy.

NICHOLAS.

    Skipps?

HUMPHREY.

           The body of Old Skipps? We'd better

    Find Tappercoom.

(HUMPHREY *exits* U. L.)

MARGARET. (*Moving to* ALIZON.)

           Alizon, what do you mean,

    Running away?

RICHARD.

             He is rather drunk. Shall I bring him

    In? He had been to see his daughter.

JENNET. (*To* THOMAS.)

               Who

    Will trouble to hang you now?

(*She crosses, exits up stairs* U. L.)

THOMAS. (*Calling after her.*)

           He couldn't lie quiet

106

Among so many bones. He had to come back
To fetch his barrow.

TAPPERCOOM. (*Enters from* U. L., *followed by* HUMPHREY.)
                    What's all this I'm told?
I was hoping to hang on my bough for the rest of the evening
Ripe and undisturbed. What is it? Murder
Not such a fabrication after all?

ALIZON.
We had to come back, you see, because nobody now
Will be able to burn her.

RICHARD.
                    Nobody will be able
To say she turned him into a dog.
(*Moving to entrance* U. R., *calling*.)
                    Come in,
Mr. Skipps.
(SKIPPS *enters from* U. R., *very unsteadily*.)

TAPPERCOOM. (*Crosses to* SKIPPS.)
                    It looks uncommonly to me
As though someone has been tampering with the evidence.
Where's Tyson?
(*Moves* L.)
                    I'm too amiable to-night
To controvert any course of events whatsoever.

SKIPPS. Your young gentleman says Come in, so I comes in. Youse
only has to say muck off, and I goes, wivout argument.

TAPPERCOOM. Splendid, of course. (*Moving a few steps toward*
SKIPPS.) Are you the rag-and-bone merchant of this town, name
of Matthew Skipps?

SKIPPS. Who give me that name? My grandfathers and grand-
mothers and all in authority undrim. Baptized I blaming was, and I
says to youse, baptized I am, and I says to youse, baptized I will be,
wiv holy weeping and washing of teeth. And immersion upon us
miserable offenders. Miserable offenders all . . . no offence meant.
And if any of youse is not a miserable offender, as he's told to be
by almight and mercerable God, then I says to him Hands off my
daughter, you bloody-minded heathen. (*Swings arm as if to hit*
someone, almost falls down, but is caught and steadied by RICHARD.
TAPPERCOOM *moves toward him*.)

TAPPERCOOM. All right, all right. . . .

107

SKIPPS. And I'm not quarrelling, mind; I'm not quarrelling. Peace on earth and good tall women. And give us our trespassers as trespassers will be prosecuted for us. I'm not perfect, mind. But I'm as good a miserable offender as any man here present, ladies excepted.

THOMAS. (*Calling to* SKIPPS *from window-seat.*) Here now, Matt, aren't you forgetting yourself? You're dead; you've been dead for hours.

SKIPPS. (*Looking at* THOMAS.) Dead am I? (*Turning to* TAPPERCOOM.) I has the respect to ask you to give me coabberation of that. I says mucking liar to nobody. But I seen my daughter three hours back, and she'd have said fair and to my face Dad, you're dead. She don't stand for no nonsense.

NICHOLAS. (RICHARD *and* ALIZON *exit* U. R.) The whole town knows it, Skipps, old man. You've been dead since this morning.

SKIPPS. Dead. Well, you take my breaf away. Do I begin to stink, then?

HUMPHREY. You do.

SKIPPS. Fair enough. That's coabberation. I'm among the blessed saints.

TAPPERCOOM. He floats in the heaven of the grape. Someone take him home to his hovel.

SKIPPS. (*Roaring, waving his arms.*) Alleluia! Alleluia! Alleluia!

TAPPERCOOM. Now, stop that, Skipps. Keep your hosannas for the cold light of morning or we shall lock you up.

SKIPPS. (*Moving about stage and singing.*) Alleluia!

TAPPERCOOM. (*To* MARGARET.) He'll wake your guests and spoil their pleasure. They're all sitting half sunk in a reef of collars. Even the dear good Chaplain has taken so many glassesful of repentance he's almost unconscious of the existence of sin.

SKIPPS. Glory, amen! Glory, glory, amen, amen!

MARGARET.

Richard will take this old man home. Richard . . .
(*Looks about for him.*)
Where is Richard? Where is Alizon?
Have they gone again?

NICHOLAS.

Yes; Humphrey's future wife,
Blown clean away.

MARGARET.

Yes; that's all very well;

108

But she mustn't think she can let herself be blown
Away whenever she likes.

THOMAS.

What better time
Than when she likes?

SKIPPS. (*Chanting.*)

As it was in the beginning,
Ever and ever, amen, al-lelulia!

MARGARET. (*To* NICHOLAS *and* HUMPHREY.)

Take the old man to his home. Now that you've made him
Think he's dead we shall never have any peace.

(NICHOLAS *and* HUMPHREY *go to* SKIPPS, *one gets on each side of him, steering him toward exit* U. R.)

HUMPHREY.

Nor shall we when he's gone.

NICHOLAS. (*Trying to get one of* SKIPPS' *arms across his shoulders so that he can support him better.*)

Spread your wings, Matthew; we're going to teach you to fly.

SKIPPS. (*Going limp, forcing* NICHOLAS *and* HUMPHREY *to support him completely.*)

I has the respect to ask to sit down.

(*To* NICHOLAS *and* HUMPHREY.)

Youse blessed saints don't
realize: it takes it out of you, this life everlasting. Alleluia!

NICHOLAS. (NICHOLAS *and* HUMPHREY *each get one of* SKIPPS' *arms over their shoulders and carry him out* U. R.)

Come on
Your second wind can blow where no one listens.

(*The three exit.*)

TAPPERCOOM.

That's more pleasant.

(*Moves* C.)

What was the thread, now, which the rascal broke?
Do I have to collect my thoughts any further?

MARGARET. (*Moving toward* TAPPERCOOM.)

Yes:
Or I must. That poor child Alizon
Is too young to go throwing herself under the wheels
Of happiness. She should have wrapped up warmly first.

(*She goes to* U. L. *door, knocks.*)

109

Hebble must know, in any case. I must tell him,
Though he's locked himself in, and only blows his nose
When I knock.

TAPPERCOOM.

                              Yes, get him on to a horse;
It will do him good.

MARGARET.

                              Hebble on a horse is a man
Delivered neck and crop to the will of God.
But he'll have to do it.

(MARGARET *crosses stage, exits up stairs,* U. L.)

TAPPERCOOM.

                              Ah yes, he'll have to do it.
He's a dear little man. . . .
(*Looking at* THOMAS.)

                              What's to be the end of you?
I take it the male prisoner is sufficiently
Deflated not to plague us with his person
Any longer?

THOMAS.

                              Deflated? I'm overblown
With the knowledge of my own villainy.

TAPPERCOOM.

                              Your guilt, my boy,
Is a confounded bore.

THOMAS.

                              Then let it bore me to extinction.

(JENNET *returns down stairs,* U. L., *wearing her own dress.*)

TAPPERCOOM. (*Crosses* U. S. C.)
The woman prisoner may notice, without
My mentioning it, that there's a certain mildness
In the night, a kind of somnolent inattention.
If she wishes to return to her cell no one
Can object. On the other hand . . . How very empty
The streets must be just now. You will forgive
A yawn in an overworked and elderly man.
(*Crosses* R.)
The moon is full, of course. To leave the town
Unobserved, one would have to use caution. As for me,
I shall go and be a burden to my bed.

110

(Going up toward door U. R.)
Good night.

JENNET.

Good night.

THOMAS.

Good night.

(Exit TAPPERCOOM U. R.)
So much for me.
(Rises and goes to get coat.)
JENNET. *(Goes up to* L. *of* THOMAS.)

Thomas, only another
Fifty years or so and then I promise
To let you go.

THOMAS.

Do you see those roofs and spires?
There sleep hypocrisy, porcous pomposity, greed,
Lust, vulgarity, cruelty, trickery, sham,
And all possible nitwittery . . . are you suggesting
Fifty years of that?

JENNET.

I was only suggesting fifty
Years of me.

THOMAS.

Girl, you haven't changed the world.
Glimmer as you will, the world's not changed.
I love you, but the world's not changed. Perhaps
I could draw you up over my eyes for a time
But the world sickens me still.

(Moves D. *to below buttress.)*
JENNET. *(Comes down with him on his* L.)

And do you think
Your gesture of death is going to change it? Except
For me?

THOMAS. *(At foot of ramp.)*

Oh, the unholy mantrap of love!

JENNET.

I have put on my own gown again.
But otherwise everything that is familiar,
My house, my poodle, peacock and possessions,
The world is looking frozen

111

And forbidding under the moon; but I must be
Out of this town before daylight comes, and somewhere,
Who knows where, begin again.

THOMAS.

Brilliant;
So you fall back on the darkness to defeat me.
You gamble of the possibility
That I was well brought up.
(Distant cock crow.)

And of course you're right.
I have to see you home, though neither of us
Knows where on earth it is.
(Crosses to her L.)

JENNET.

Thomas, can you mean to let
The world go on?

THOMAS.

I know my limitations.
When the landscape goes to seed, the wind is obsessed
By to-morrow.
(Cock crow sounds near.)

JENNET.

I shall have to hurry.
That was the pickaxe voice of the cock, beginning
To break up the night. Am I an inconvenience
To you?

THOMAS.

As inevitable as original sin.
(Puts coat around her and kisses her.)
And I shall be loath to forgo one day of you,
Even for the sake of my ultimate friendly death.

JENNET.

I am friendly too.

THOMAS.

Then let me wish us both
Good morning. And God have mercy on our souls!
(Distant cock crow. They move off together toward door U. R. as)

CURTAIN FALLS

PROPERTY LIST

ACT I

Bread (Nicholas)
Book
Paper
Quill pen
Ink stamp
Horoscope (piece of paper)
Bunch of daffodils
Viol (old instrument like a small cello. Violin can be substituted)
Handkerchief
Workbasket with sewing materials in it
Prayer books
Music (on large "parchment")
Bunch of keys

ACT II

Fire tongs
Small lantern
Various papers on desk
Handkerchief (large)
Bucket, floor cloth, knee pad

ACT III

Beer barrel
Jewel box
Tankard (empty)
Clothes, etc., tied in handkerchief
Five bottles of wine